English Lit Relit

A short history of English literature from the Precursors
(before swearing) to the Pre-Raphaelites and a
little after, intended to help students see the
thing through, or see through the thing,
and omitting nothing unimportant

by
Richard Armour

Irreverently illustrated by
Campbell Grant

McGraw-Hill Book Company
New York · Toronto · London

DEDICATED

to anyone who, having given or taken
an English Survey course, can truthfully state,
"I am monarch of all I survey."

Contents

I

The Anglo-Saxon Period

ONE cannot fully understand English literature without knowing something of the land and the people from which that literature has sprung. England is a small island,[1] on most maps about three inches long and two inches wide, full of people with hyphenated names because of their Anglo-Saxon background. They can be recognized by their broad a's. The rainfall is heavy, especially on week ends. The countryside is rolling, as is noticed by anyone who has ever landed after a rough crossing on the Channel.

"The blood of the original inhabitants," we are told, "was mixed with that of the Celts, Romans, Angles, Saxons, Jutes, Danes, and Normans." Precisely when this stirring event occurred we do not know, but it must have been a gruesome ceremony, perhaps influencing Shakespeare's description of the witches and their caldron in *Macbeth*.

English literature began with the coming of the Angles and Saxons to England in 449 A.D. The Jutes,

[1] Or part of an island, depending on how seriously you take Scotland and Wales. England is often compared with Alabama, but only with regard to size.

who came with them and were tall, upright people, seem not to have had a literary bent. Before these tribes arrived in England, English was German and English literature was therefore German literature. The Angles and the Saxons were good friends. The Angles knew all the Saxons, and the Saxons, who were clever people, knew all the Angles. Anglo-Saxon, or Old English, had a guttural sound, since it was Low German and not far removed from the guttur. It was also highly infected.

Old English poetry was oral, and it was therefore no disgrace to be an unpublished poet. Instead of being written down it was recited by a scop or bard who went about from court to court. This was not because he was always breaking the law but because he knew only so many poems by heart and was kept on the move by noble lords and ladies who greeted his recitation with cries of "We've heard that one before" and "No, not again!"

The early bards depended greatly on alliteration, and would have envied such a lilting line as "Peter Piper picked a peck of pickled peppers." The best they could do was something like "Canst thou not, comrade, ken that knife?" [1]

Caedmon

The first English poet whose name has survived was Caedmon. Caedmon was a bashful swineherd who would slink out of parties before it was his turn to tell a story. He could never think of anything that would come up to the stories the other swineherds told, and envied their wit and *savoir-faire*.

One night, when he had slipped outside to avoid being called on, he went to the stables and fell asleep and had a vision. In the vision Someone told him what to say, and the next night Caedmon, with his Holy Ghost-written poem, was the life of the party. Once started, there was no stopping him, until he was finally shut up in a monastery. Not until Byron did another English poet wake up to find himself famous.

Beowulf

Beowulf was found in a cotton manuscript in the British Museum, full of kennings. Its author is unknown, and this has led to several interesting theories. One is

[1] Be sure to pronounce the "k" in "knife" to get the full poetic effect.

that the author kept his name a secret, after he realized what he had written, for the sake of his family. Another is that there was not a single author but many authors, which would account for the length of the poem.[1] Still another theory is that there was no author, and the whole thing was a hoax, dreamed up by English professors who had to have something with which to begin Sophomore Survey.

The poem is considered an epic because of its long speeches, its digressions, its repetition, its bloodshed, and its being required. It is given unity by a hero, in this instance Beowulf, who was no ordinary man. For one thing, he had the strength of thirty men, and the one thing he had all this strength for was to get the better of monsters who were pretty strong themselves. Though scholars argue violently over many points, they are in agreement on essentials, such as the fact that the poem runs to 3182 lines.

Beowulf was a noble hero. He fought the wicked sea monster, Grendel, with his bare hands, disdaining gloves. Then, when he had torn off Grendel's arm, instead of keeping it as a souvenir he generously hung it over the doorway to Hrothgar's hall so that all might enjoy it. Later he also gave Grendel's head to Hrothgar, apparently knowing Hrothgar liked that sort of thing. Fortunately Beowulf finally went back to his homeland, else Hrothgar's hall, Heorot, would have been full of bits and pieces. Beowulf even went so far as to kill Grendel's mother, which some might consider

[1] Ettmüller, Müllenhoff, and Möller, German scholars of the Umlaut School, believe that there were not only several authors but several poems. *Beowulf* may thus have been the first anthology.

Beowulf

A noble hero

ungentlemanly, but this was before the Age of Chivalry. Besides, this underwater witch had slain the king's thane.[1]

Beowulf has little of the comic in it.[2] Those who are easily depressed by brutal killings, dire deeds of vengeance, and scenery full of dark shadows and fogs and unwholesome vapors may go so far as to call it gloomy. One critic has said that "It breathes the air of the tomb." It is something, though, for a poem to breathe at all.

Other Writings

Most other Old English poetry is in the form of laments and complaints. Apparently poets were getting along no better in those days than today, or were hard to please. One poet whose name is known is Cynewulf, and the reason his name is known is that he wrote it right into his poems by means of runes. Some think this runed his work, but his name is secure.

---

[1] What a pity Grendel didn't paint. A somewhat idealized portrait, entitled "Grendel's Mother," would be the showpiece of any gallery.

[2] It does have what is called "grim Anglo-Saxon humor." Warriors held their sides—not because of laughter but because of sword thrusts.

II

The Middle English Period

THE Norman Conquest brought French ideas into English literature, and what the French had most on their minds was romance.[1] However it was a Welshman, King Arthur, who outdid them all. As one scholar says, "The romances of Arthur far outnumber the others in England." Despite the prowess of Arthur, he had to watch his queen, Guinevere, and his handsome young knights, such as Lancelot. To keep his eye on them better, he made them all sit at a round table.

[1] Later known as sex.

Brought French ideas

Sir Gawain and the Green Knight

One of Arthur's knights was Sir Gawain, who once had a rather unusual experience. A strange knight, dressed all in green and riding a green horse,[1] offered to let Gawain hit him with an ax if he could do the same to Gawain a year and a day later. This seemed fair enough, and Gawain took him up on it, because a year and a day is a long time and anything might happen in the interval. Then with one blow of his ax Gawain cut off the green knight's head. The green knight picked up his head, as soon as it stopped rolling, and rode off laughing (out of his neck or somewhere).

On his way, none too rapidly, to find the green knight and get the blow that was coming to him, Gawain stayed at a roadside castle. Each day, while the lord of the castle was out hunting, the lord's wife came into Gawain's bedroom and tempted him mightily. All

[1] Green colored, not inexperienced.

Tempted him mightily

Gawain took was a few harmless kisses until the final day, when he accepted a girdle from the lady rather than hurt her feelings. The girdle was supposed to protect him from harm, and Gawain thought it would come in handy when he faced the green knight. Meanwhile it would hold in his stomach.

As it turned out, the green knight was the lady's husband, and it was he who had told her to tempt Gawain.[1] After swinging the ax several times, the green knight finally nicked Gawain's neck, that being for his taking the girdle. The whole thing had been a test, and Gawain had got an A–. The moral of the story is that it's all right to kiss the lady of the house when her husband is away but you shouldn't carry off any of her undergarments.[2]

Middle English Songs

"The English people," we are told, "kept singing all through the turbulent seven centuries from Caedmon to Chaucer." This is a long time to keep singing, and it is no wonder the Middle Ages became known as the age of the hoarse. It was hard to get a song in edgewise.[3]

An example of a song of this period is the one beginning

[1] Telling your wife to do something like this is risky, and not recommended to most husbands.

[2] Some scholars believe the girdle in the poem is connected with creation of the Order of the Garter. Possibly the order started a little higher up and gradually slipped.

[3] With the Hundred Years' War, the Black Death, and the Peasants' Revolt, things were humming.

> Sumer is icumen in,
> Lhude sing cuccu.

This is the type of song known as a round, and it has been around a long time. Critics admire its freshness and simplicity, as well as the inventiveness shown in the spelling of "loud" as "lhude." [1]

One of the most exciting features of the song in the Middle Ages is that many English songsters were bilingual or even trilingual, meaning they had two or three tongues. This enabled them to sing several songs at once.

The most popular song was the love lyric, such as the one beginning

> Blow, northerne wynd,
> Send thou me my sueting!

The poet is asking the wind to blow his love to him, and one can almost see her borne on the gale. She is a little on the plump side, as the word "sueting" reveals, and the wind may have to huff and puff to get her moving, but she will make a soft landing.

Geoffrey Chaucer

Passing over Wyclif, Gower, Langland, and other writers, as well as the morality plays (they really weren't all that moral), we come to Geoffrey Chaucer.

[1] Of course it may mean "lewd," the medieval cuckoo knowing some pretty risqué songs.

Despite his trouble with spelling, Chaucer was the greatest writer of the fourteenth century. He was bookish from his youth, starting out as a page. When he was in his twenties he married a lady-in-waiting who had been lying in wait for him. At one time he was controller of customs in London, customs apparently having got out of control. But he got most of his material for writing when the King appointed him inspector of the sewers along the Thames. What he reported to the King is not known, but he saw some things that had to wait more than five centuries to be written about. Finally, near the end of his life, he took a house next door to Westminster Abbey. He wanted to be handy if he should be tapped for Poets' Corner.[1]

Many of Chaucer's poems, such as *The Book of the Duchess, The House of Fame,* and *The Legend of*

[1] Chaucer was about sixty when he took a fifty-three-year lease on the house. Then he settled back, feeling reasonably secure.

Good Women, are in the form of a dream. The poet goes to sleep at the beginning of the poem and doesn't wake up until the end, and the same thing happens to many students. Chaucer also left several of his works unfinished, perhaps getting a little tired of them himself. Or something may have come up, such as his suddenly remembering an appointment with the doctor for his Black Death inoculations, and when he got back to his desk he wasn't in the mood.

Chaucer's greatest complete work is *Troilus and Criseyde,* which is about Troilus and Criseyde.

His best-known work, however, is *The Canterbury Tales,* and the best-known part of this is the Prologue, especially the first line. Almost everyone can (and does) quote "Whan that Aprille with his shoures soote," followed by "and so forthe." Some of the tales, such as the Miller's and the Reeve's, are so rough, bawdy, and low class that they have universal appeal. But there are also tales of tenderness and high morality. As one critic has said, "There is a wide range between coarse and fine," suggesting that Chaucer wrote not with a pen but with a sieve.

If you picture the Wife of Bath going around with a cake of soap and a towel, you have the wrong idea.

III

The Elizabethan Period

BEFORE coming to the great writers of the Elizabethan Period, let us look briefly at two important literary forms, the popular ballad and the sonnet.

The popular ballad is known for its refrain, which is intended to warn the reader against going any further. An example of a refrain is the memorable line, "Fa la la la fa la la la ra re." A noteworthy development came in the famous ballad "Edward," where the refrain is skilfully varied, alternating between "Edward, Edward" and "Mither, mither." [1] But probably the high point of balladry was reached in "The Three Ravens," the opening stanza of which goes:

> There were three ravens sat on a tree,
> > Downe a downe, hay down, hay downe
> There were three ravens sat on a tree,
> > With a downe
> There were three ravens sat on a tree,
> They were as blacke as they might be.
> > With a downe derrie, derrie, derrie,
> > downe, downe.

[1] Edward calls his mother "mither," a combination of "mother" and "wither." She was apparently a dried-up old lady.

Ravens with a downe

What is remarkable about this is that if the reader fails to get the idea from the first line that three ravens sat on a tree, he has two more chances. Moreover there is a sense of mystery, often found in the ballad, when we are left to wonder whether the three ravens sat on a tree with a downe, which is a soft, downy bird (making four birds in all), or simply sat downe on a tree. The mystery is deepened by the word "derrie," which may mean "dearie," thus introducing the love element, or *"derrière,"* indicating what it was the ravens sat downe on and suggesting a borrowing from the French.[1]

The sonnet was introduced into English poetry by Wyatt and Surrey, sometimes thought to be one man called Wyatt N. Surrey. The most important thing about the sonnet is its having exactly fourteen lines, and the first step in any critical study is to count the lines. If a poet can't get everything he wants to say into fourte

[1] There has been little borrowing from the French since the Middle Ages. However a downe derrie, or a downy *derrière*, is very French.

lines, he puts what is left over into another sonnet. Most of the early sonnets were about love and were addressed to mistresses, poets having learned that a poem will soften up a girl fully as well as a ring or a bracelet.

There are two kinds of sonnets, the Italian or Petrarchan and the English or Shakespearean. The first may be recognized by its opening lines, "Abba, abba," while the second starts out "Ab, ab." One critic has said that "a sonnet is to an ode as a cameo is to a monument." [1] If you hold a cameo up next to a monument you will see what he has in mind.

Sir Philip Sidney

The Elizabethans believed in gallantry and good manners, and Sir Philip Sidney was their ideal. In Elizabeth's court, no one was courtier.

According to his biographer, "On both sides he was an aristocrat," and we assume this was also true front and rear, since he was a well-rounded gentleman. Those who think the sonnet cycle, which Sidney invented, was a means of transportation will be disappointed to learn that his was a series of 108 sonnets, written to another man's wife. [2] Another work, his *Arcadia*, is sometimes called the first novel in English. A little reading about the adventures of the two young knights, Musidorus

[1] I misread this at first, thinking it was "as a camel is to a monument," perhaps one of the pyramids.

[2] A less plausible theory, in view of their passionate nature, is that they were addressed to his own wife.

Sir Philip Sidney

and Pyrocles, will suggest how far the novel was to go in the hands of Fielding and Dickens. It is a pastoral romance—the kind of love story a pastor could read without blushing.

Sidney was embarrassed about some of the poems he wrote, and in one of the sonnets tells of "Biting my truant pen, beating myself for spite." Many authors have felt like doing something of the sort but have been unable to go through with it, perhaps for fear of breaking a tooth. Sidney tried to make amends in his *Apologie for Poetrie*, but the damage was already done.

He died heroically at the battle of Zutphen, declining a cup of water and letting another soldier have it. This has been praised for centuries as an act of chivalry, though there are some who think Sidney wasn't thirsty.

Sir Walter Raleigh

Sir Walter Raleigh was a soldier, poet, historian, courtier, explorer, and businessman.[1] He made a great impression on Queen Elizabeth by spreading his cape over a mud puddle. She saw at once that here was a man with imagination and utter disdain for cleaning bills. He was in and out of favor with the Queen. When he was out of favor he was in the Tower and when he was in favor he was out of the Tower. Queen Elizabeth was annoyed when he named one of the places he settled

[1] Busy as he was, he obviously lacked the time to revise the poem *His Pilgrimage*. I have in mind the line about wells where something sweet is "Drawn up by saints in crystal buckets." Did the saints draw up the sweet stuff or were the saints in the crystal buckets? We shall never know for sure.

Out of favor

Virginia instead of Elizabeth, but Raleigh got himself out of that one by saying he was complimenting her, the Virgin Queen. The Queen started to say, "Who, me?" but caught herself and let it pass. Raleigh was quick witted and the Queen wasn't stupid.

Raleigh was imprisoned for thirteen years by James I. This gave him ample leisure to write. "What can I write that will take me thirteen years?" he asked himself. Very wisely he chose to write a *History of the World*. This was better than keeping track of the years by marks on the wall. When finally he was executed, he is said to have joked with his executioner, making hilarious remarks about chips off the old chopping block and all that sort of thing. The executioner nearly died laughing until he realized he wasn't the one to go. "You axed for it," he said, answering quip for quip. It was a fun afternoon.

Edmund Spenser

Edmund Spenser is known as the poet's poet. Spenser's favorite poet was Chaucer, who was therefore the poet's poet's poet.[1] One of Spenser's early works was his *Shepherd's Calendar*. Fortunately time meant little to shepherds, because they could never have figured out the day of the week from it. But the poem gives the reader a good idea of the shepherd's life: sitting around all day talking in verse about women, poetry, and the classic myths, while the flock wandered at will. Colin

[1] One hesitates to mention it, but Spenser's favorite poet may have been Spenser. This still would make him the poet's poet.

E. Spenser

Clout and his friends stayed out of doors day after day, rain or shine, and gradually became rustic.

Spenser's greatest work was *The Faerie Queene*. It is one of the longest poems in English, and anyone who says he has read every word of it is not to be trusted. Even then, Spenser wrote only about half of what he had planned, for which students can be grateful. As he explains in his letter to Sir Walter Raleigh, the beginning of the poem was to have been in the twelfth book, which he never got to. The poem is therefore unusual in going for thousands of lines without ever starting.

The Faerie Queene is full of meaning, since everything not only means what it means but also means something else. The Red Cross Knight, for instance, means holiness, and the Fairy Queen means Queen

Elizabeth, to whom the poem is dedicated. The Queen reacted to all this about as Spenser expected, giving him a pension.[1] The poem maintains a delicate balance. For every lady in distress there is a champion to rescue her, and for every fiery dragon there is someone to put out the fire by cutting off the dragon's head.

Interest is aroused at once by the first line, "A gentle Knight was pricking on the plaine," because one wonders what or whom he is pricking. Soon one learns it is his horse and his horse is angry, which is understandable. Though Spenser usually writes delicately and with good taste, he gives the reader hope, early in the poem, when he refers to the lovely lady with "an asse more white than snow." It is this same lady who coaches the Red Cross Knight, when the loathsome serpent Error has wrapped him in her tail. "Strangle her," she says, "else she sure will strangle thee." [2] The lady does not tell the knight how to manage this, pinned down as he is, but it is excellent advice, setting a precedent for spectators at wrestling matches.

It is a great poem, full of conceits (there was nothing modest about Spenser) and clashing symbols.[3]

[1] Spenser was disappointed, however. He had expected more. Unfortunately for Spenser they didn't pay by the line in those days.

[2] And she sure would have.

[3] The poem is written in the Spenserian stanza. There was something about the name of this poetic form that appealed to Spenser.

Christopher Marlowe

Among the university wits, who kept Cambridge laughing, was Christopher Marlowe. When he and the others left the university and went to London, the professors were at their wits' end.

Marlowe was both a poet and a dramatist. As a poet he wrote the beautiful lyric beginning "Come live with me and be my love," in which a passionate shepherd promises all sorts of things, such as a cap of flowers and a rather flimsy belt made out of straw and ivy buds, if the girl will move in with him. We shall never know whether she accepted on these terms or waited for something a little more solid, such as an offer of marriage.

Passionate shepherd

As a dramatist **Marlowe**, according to one critic, "stands next to Shakespeare." He is the one at the left with a glass in his hand. Marlowe's plays include *Tamburlaine*, *The Jew of Malta*, *Edward II*, and *Dr. Faustus*. Tamburlaine, the hero of his first play, was "larger than life" and had to be divided into two parts. There are ten acts in *Tamburlaine*. On the other hand there are no acts in *Dr. Faustus*, but there is plenty of talk. Dr. Faustus is a talented young man who sells his soul to the Devil and thereafter goes downhill so steadily that it is easy to see where he will wind up. It is in *Dr. Faustus* that Marlowe asks the famous question:

> Was this the face that launch'd a thousand ships
> And burnt the topless towers of Ilium? [1]

Marlowe is not referring to Dr. Faustus' face, which was all right but hardly capable of launching a ship or starting a fire. Indeed that seems a good deal to ask of any face, however versatile.

When he was only twenty-nine, Marlowe got into a tavern brawl and was stabbed in the fracas.

William Shakespeare

The greatest of the Elizabethan writers was William Shakespeare. What made him so great was that he managed to get Bacon, Marlowe, and the Earl of Oxford to write his plays for him. Meanwhile, during the Lost Years, he was trying to find himself.

[1] Topless towers are not so indecent as they sound.

Shakespeare was born in Stratford-on-Avon, the son of a glover. He is thought to have modeled children's gloves (kid gloves) for his father. At any rate he worked hand in glove with his old man, though he became furious when smart alecks passing the shop taunted him, calling him "glover boy." Soon he married Anne Hathaway, whom he met when he was with a group of tourists visiting Anne Hathaway's Cottage. He was eighteen and she was twenty-six, and when people lifted their eyebrows he said, "What's the difference?" The difference was eight years, as anyone could have told him but few did. All we know of his married life is that when she gave birth to twins, Shakespeare left Stratford and went to London. He had had it.[1] The name of one of the twins, Hamnet, gave him the idea for a play.[2]

[1] Actually Anne had had it (or them).

[2] Some think Shakespeare left Stratford because he was caught poaching a deer, perhaps over an open fire.

Shakespeare began his theatrical career as a call boy, which is different from a call girl, and then progressed to actor and finally part owner of a theatrical company and of the Globe Theater. He made so much money that he bought one of the finest homes in Stratford, called a showplace because of the source of the money. The house had ten fireplaces, Shakespeare vowing never to be cold again.

Over Shakespeare's grave is an inscription that says: "Curst be he that moves my bones." So far as is known, the bones have never been moved. People who visit the grave are curious, but they are waiting for someone else to make the first move. Besides, visitors are permitted cameras but not picks and shovels.

Shakespeare's plays are divided into three types: histories, tragedies, and comedies. Some critics add two other kinds: good and bad. The tragedies end with the

Killed or crowned

principal characters stabbed or poisoned. The histories end with the principal characters killed or crowned. The comedies, which often have a tragic element, end with the principal characters married.

Shakespeare borrowed his plots. He would edge up to a playwright on a London street and say, "Could you lend me a fiver?" (Meaning a five-act plot.) Mostly, however, he borrowed plots from writers who were dead and would not be after him to get them back.

His characters are memorable. Who can forget Valeria in *Coriolanus* or Pisanio in *Cymbeline* or, for that matter, the Messenger in *Titus Andronicus?* Then there are his famous lines, such as the oft-quoted "Is it near dinner time?" spoken by Julia in *Two Gentlemen of Verona*, and the stirring "Hold, villain!" uttered by the First Pirate in *Pericles*. For spare, taut dialogue, nothing surpasses this interchange[1] in *Troilus and Cressida*:

Patroclus. Jove bless great Ajax!

Thersites. Hum!

Patrocles. I come from the worthy Achilles,—

Thersites. Ha!

Patrocles. Who most humbly desires you to invite Hector to his tent,—

Thersites. Hum!

Thersites was not only a man of few words but of few syllables. And notice with what artistry Shakespeare brings in the "Ha!" when we are expecting another "Hum!" Shakespeare is never content with the ordinary.

---

[1] In which Patroclus is shortchanged.

One of Shakespeare's most effective dramatic devices is the soliloquy, when a character talks to himself but you are able to hear him if he speaks distinctly and you aren't sitting too far back. He also uses comic relief, as in *King Lear*, when the Fool is forever jesting. The Fool says hilarious things, even as Lear goes mad and wanders around in a storm, Gloucester's eyes are put out, Cordelia is hanged, Edgar kills Edmund, and Goneril poisons Regan and then stabs herself. But for the Fool's witticisms, such as when he calls the King "nuncle," it might be a rather serious play.

In addition to his plays Shakespeare wrote two narrative poems and CLIV sonnets. One group of the sonnets is about a dark lady, but we are left in the dark about who she is.[1]

Ben Jonson

Ben Jonson was once a bricklayer, which explains references to his "solid achievement" and his having "built on a firm foundation." He was a strong, burly fellow and quick to anger. "Twice he killed his man in single combat," writes one biographer, not explaining why Jonson thought it necessary to kill the poor fellow more than once. He must have been angry indeed.

Many of Ben Jonson's plays are based on the idea that people are composed of four humors: blood, phlegm, bile, and black bile. According to Jonson's

---

[1] In that scholarly work, *Twisted Tales from Shakespeare*, the author points out that another group of sonnets is addressed to a young man, or "dark laddy."

theory a person with too much phlegm would be phlegmatic, though the doctor would probably call it a hard cold and prescribe two aspirin.

Jonson's perceptiveness is nowhere more apparent than in the names he chose for some of his characters, such as Fastidious Brisk in *Every Man Out of His Humor,* Sir Politick Would-Be in *Volpone,* Sir Epicure Mammon in *The Alchemist,* and Zeal-of-the-Land Busy in *Bartholomew Fair.* Most of Jonson's plays are set in London and he must have spent many hours looking through the phone book for unusual names for his characters.

In addition to his plays Jonson wrote masques. These are court entertainments full of singing, dancing, and mumming.[1] One of his most exciting masques is

[1] An evening of mumming has been called a dumb show by disgruntled critics.

Oberon, which opens in pitch darkness and might have been even more interesting had it remained that way. The high point of the masque is when Oberon descends in a bear-drawn chariot. The fays, satyrs, and other onlookers are spellbound, never having seen a bear-drawn chariot before, and remain under the spell until dawn, when they have one last dance (one for the road) and head for home.[1]

Jonson never lived up to his promise, made in *Every Man Out of His Humor:*

> I'll strip the ragged follies of the time,
> Naked, as at their birth.

Had he done so, he would have anticipated Ziegfeld and Minsky by three hundred years.

Over Jonson's grave in Westminster Abbey is the inscription "O rare Ben Jonson." What was so unusual about Ben was that he was buried vertically, to save space. His position in Westminster Abbey, if not in English literature, is secure.

Francis Bacon

Francis Bacon's father was Lord Keeper of the Great Seal, a sinecure that probably involved only throwing it a little food at mealtimes. Bacon himself held many positions under Queen Elizabeth, and at one time was Lord Keeper. Keeping lords, however, was no easy job, a kept lord making even more demands than a kept

[1] The audience had already gone.

woman. When he was Attorney-General, he made the mistake of taking presents from persons whose cases were pending before him, and, still worse, of being caught. Bacon protested, "I never had bribe or reward in my eye or thought." [1] He did not deny, however, that he put the money in his wallet.

Having been caught accepting bribes, Bacon was more than ever convinced of the importance of knowledge. "If only they hadn't *known*," he muttered to himself. In *The Advancement of Learning* he disposes of the objections to learning, such as the fact that it is hard work and cuts into the time otherwise given to recreation. He also tells of the advantages, for example knowing more than someone else and feeling superior. As for himself, "I have taken all knowledge to be my province," he once declared, which was another way of saying that he intended to specialize in everything.

Bacon's best-known writings are his *Essays*. They are loved for many reasons, such as their being so short. The title of each of the fifty-eight essays begins with "Of," which gives unity to the collection. The essays are full of common sense and good advice, as in "Of Expense," when Bacon says, "Riches are for spending," a thought that occurred to him when he was hitting up a wealthy friend for a loan. Or in "Of Building," when he sagely remarks, "Houses are built to live in." This came to him in a moment of inspiration, and the more you think of it the better it seems than, say, "Houses are built to pay taxes on."

[1] Apparently his accusers suspected him of stashing cash in the bags under his eyes.

Bacon, who had a scientific turn of mind, was always experimenting. Once he became fascinated with echoes, trying to keep sounds from coming back or hoping to yell one thing and have something different respond, so he could keep up more of a conversation. His most exciting discovery was when, as he says, "I did hap to find that an echo would not return S, being but a hissing and interior sound." You can try this for yourself, hissing and then listening until the men in white come for you and carry you away. Bacon's last experiment was when he stuffed a chicken with snow, on a cold, raw day in early spring, to see whether the chicken would keep. The experiment was a success, but Bacon caught a chill and died within a week. What this proves is that chicken, when stuffed with snow, keeps better than Bacon.

Elizabethan Lyrics

England was known at this time as "a nation of singing birds." Everyone was a-twitter. Consider John Lyly's song about a card game, something like strip poker, played by Cupid and Campaspe. Cupid lost the coral of his lip, the rose growing on his cheek,[1] and the dimple in his chin. Finally he tossed his eyes on the table in a last desperate chance and lost these also. He was wiped out, and Campaspe went home with a handbag full of somewhat unusual winnings.

Then there is the rather naughty song,[2] "Back and side, go bare, go bare," with its haunting lines,

> I cannot eat but little meat,
> My stomach is not good.[3]

For true jollity one has only to turn to Samuel Daniel's "Love is a sickness full of woes" or John Fletcher's "Lay a garland on my hearse." However let us conclude this discussion of the lyrics of the Elizabethan Period, indeed sum up the literature of this era, with something more typical, the delightful refrain in Thomas Nash's "Spring":

> Cuckoo, jug-jug, pu-we, to-witta-woo!

---

[1] See Thomas Campion's "There is a garden in her face." People grew flowers and vegetables in the most unlikely places in those days.

[2] Anonymous, and no wonder.

[3] The poet was really upset.

IV

Seventeenth-Century Poetry

WRITERS of the seventeenth century fall into two groups, the Cavaliers or Roundheads and the Puritans or Squareheads. The Cavaliers believed in having a good time now, in case now is all there is. The Puritans believed in waiting for the Hereafter, which would last

A good time now

longer. Middle-of-the-roaders had a good time all week, but went to church on Sunday.

John Donne

John Donne is hard to classify. In fact he is often hard to understand. Dr. Johnson called him "metaphysical," which seems as good a term as any, especially when you learn that metaphysical means "of or pertaining to metaphysics."

"After a secular youth," we are told, "Donne took orders at the age of forty-three." He had been terribly secular, fooling around with the girls and all that, and

Terribly secular

for a long time no one could order *him* around, especially his parents. He secretly married Anne More, and his father-in-law was so angry when he found out that he had Donne put in prison and didn't give him a wedding present. Later, in a tribute to his wife, who bore him twelve children, Donne coined an epigram: "John Donne—Anne Donne—undone." It would have made a nice inscription on a bracelet.[1]

In view of some of the sexy poems Donne wrote, it is hard to imagine him Dean of St. Paul's. He must have been one of the "poetic cannons," hot as a pistol, referred to by literary historians. Among his poems is the one in which he tells the reader to "Go and catch a falling star," "Get with child a mandrake root," and do other things that most would find difficult. The critic was right who said, "Donne makes demands on his readers."[2]

Donne's poetry has to be read carefully. It is hard to scan. One who tried to scan it was Ben Jonson, who said that for not keeping the accent Donne deserved hanging. In those days people were hanged or had their heads chopped off for considerably less than getting an iamb and a trochee mixed up.[3]

Love and death were much on Donne's mind. He had an eye for the women, his poems being full of figures. "I can love both fair and brown," he says in one

[1] Actually it was Anne who was undone. She died at thirty-two, unable to bear any more.

[2] Donne could also be pretty irritable, as when he said, "For God's sake hold your tongue, and let me love." Apparently someone had walked in and started chattering when Donne was busy.

[3] In a line of poetry Donne sometimes got off on the wrong foot.

poem, indicating his all-embracing nature. As for death, he posed in his shroud for the monument to be placed over his tomb. He wanted people to know how he looked without having to peek inside.

George Herbert

Of the religious poets, George Herbert was one of the most pious. Charles I, we are told, "gave him the living of Fugglestone," which sounds devilish and full of interesting possibilities. But instead of living it up, Herbert held services twice a day in the church, helped the poor, and spent his spare time playing the violin. If he thought he was setting an example for poets, he was deluding himself.[1]

[1] See Byron, Shelley, and other poets who gave their biographers more to write about. The editor of George Herbert's works, by the way, is George Herbert Palmer, an intriguing coincidence.

G. Herbert

of Fugglestone

Herbert had his moments. In *The Collar* he cries out:

> I struck the board, and cried, "No more;
>   I will abroad!
> What! shall I ever sigh and pine?
> My lines and life are free; free as the road,
>   Loose as the wind, and large as store.
>   Shall I be still in suit?"

But when he got as far as that last line, thinking about taking off his clothes, he remembered he was a clergyman and began to calm down.[1]

Herbert died of consumption from living in a house with a leaky roof. He thought of telling someone of the condition of the place, but shrank from saying such a thing as "This damp house."[2]

Robert Herrick

A very different sort of person was Robert Herrick, a Cavalier poet though also a vicar. His complex personality may have resulted from his unusual lineage. As one literary historian says, "Herrick was a direct descendant of Anacreon, Horace, Catullus, and Ben Jonson."

Herrick wrote so much about brooks and streams that he became known for his fluid verse.[3] He also loved

---

[1] What caused this outburst is unclear. Perhaps Herbert had been wearing a collar a size too small and could stand it no longer.

[2] Izaak Walton wrote a biography of Herbert, thinking him a queer fish.

[3] It is also called limpid, perhaps because it limps a little.

flowers. At the opening of his *Hesperides* he says he is going to tell "How roses first came red, and lilies white." As he explains it,

> Roses at first were white,
>   Till they could not agree,
> Whether my Sapho's breast
>   Or they more white should be.
>
> But being vanquished quite,
>   A blush their cheeks bespread;
> Since when, believe the rest,
>   The roses first came red.

This is an interesting explanation, but botanists say it is unscientific.[1]

"Gather ye rosebuds while ye may," Herrick says in another poem, still unable to get roses and Sapho's white breast out of his mind. But soon he begins to think of Julia, Anthea, Electra, Myrha, Perilla, Corinna, and others who had their good points too. The only trouble with Corinna was that it was hard to get her out of bed in the morning when it was time to go a-Maying. While Herrick beat on the door and shouted things like "Get up, get up for shame!" and "Get up, sweet slug-a-bed!" and tried to tempt her with such sights as "The dew bespangled herb and tree," Corinna either mumbled "Go away" or kept still and hoped he would think her not at home. Corinna had to get her beauty sleep, if she was to be worth describing in poems.

[1] It would be an interesting laboratory experiment, holding a bunch of white roses up close to a girl's breast and waiting for them to turn red.

To round out the picture of Herrick, you should know that he trained a pet pig to drink from a tankard. "Watch me," he kept saying, until finally the pig got the idea.

Herrick and friend

Other Lyrists

Let us look briefly at a few minor seventeenth-century writers of lyrics. Consider George Wither, aptly named because of his "Shall I, wasting in despair?" He wasted slowly, however, living until he was almost eighty, a dried-up little old man. And Henry Vaughan, who once remarked, in a casual, offhand manner, "I saw Eternity the other night." The ordinary person would have been more excited, phoning the police or calling a press conference. There was also Thomas Carew, who finally grew tired of being asked stupid questions, such as what does Jove do with faded roses and where do falling stars wind up and where does the

Phoenix build its nest. "Ask me no more," he said, and there was a wild look in his eyes. And then there was Edmund Waller, remembered for his *On a Girdle,* which opens:

> That which her tender waist confined
> Shall now my joyful temples bind.

Waller may have thought it helped his headache, squeezing the blood vessels, or he may just have been clowning.

Two better known lyrists are Sir John Suckling and Richard Lovelace, both of them Cavalier poets. It was a good thing they enjoyed life when they did, because both died young, Suckling committing suicide and Lovelace dying "in the poverty which loyalty had brought in its train." [1]

---

[1] A freight train, no doubt.

Suckling is known for his

> Out upon it, I have loved
> > Three whole days together!
> And am like to love three more,
> > If it prove fair weather.

It is not clear why he couldn't have kept going just as well or better if it rained, unless he did his loving outdoors. He also wrote:

> Why so pale and wan, fond lover?
> Prithee, why so pale?

It is strange he should have asked this question. Had he himself looked in the mirror after three straight days of loving, he would have seen that this sort of thing is debilitating.

Lovelace wrote those famous lines:

> Stone walls do not a prison make,
> Nor iron bars a cage.

Jailed for political offences, he had spent enough time in prison, beating on the walls and tugging at the bars, to know better. Or perhaps he had gone stir crazy. His fellow prisoners shook their heads. *They* knew what was keeping them in.

John Milton

The greatest writer of the seventeenth century was John Milton. As he himself says, he wrote poetry with his right hand and prose with his left hand, turning out

words at a great rate. After seven years at Christ's College, Cambridge, and gaining a master's degree, Milton settled down to five years of studying on his own, thinking it time to learn something. He was known at Cambridge as "the lady of Christ's," which was a somewhat misleading nickname, since he later married three times.[1] As all of the women in his life knew, he believed in a free press (or squeeze). He also believed in the divine right of kings to be executed.

L'Allegro and *Ill Penseroso* are about a happy man and a man who is sick. What is really remarkable about the two poems is that they begin with the same word

[1] Better than average for a Puritan.

("hence") and end with the same word ("live"). This makes them companion poems and almost inseparable.

Lycidas is a pastoral allergy about the death of a college friend, Edward King. The official report said he died of drowning, but some think he was bucolic. Then again, the reference to "his watery bier" may indicate that he drank too much.[1] Milton and his friend were very close. "For we were nursed upon the self-same hill," Milton says, the two mothers apparently sitting there with their infants, looking down on the valley and chatting the while. Later the lads were shepherds together, battening their flocks (with a special type of bat used by shepherds) and singing rural ditties. Though Milton at first laments the death of his friend, he comes to the conclusion that he is not really dead but gone to another place where "With nectar pure his oozy locks he laves," at last getting that pesky cowlick to stay down.

Skipping over *Comus, Samson Agonistes,* and the sonnets, which, fortunately, are beyond the scope of this brief survey, we come to *Paradise Lost.* Milton's purpose in this poem was to justify the ways of God to men, even he being unable to write a poem long enough to justify the ways of men to God or of men to men.[2] *Paradise Lost* begins in the middle of things, and for a while it is the reader who is lost. Soon it appears that Satan, who had been living in Heaven, went to Hell. With him went his "infernal peers," who were always looking around unpleasantly. The Miltonic style is

[1] Or it may explain why he drowned himself.
[2] As it is, *Paradise Lost* is pretty long, being an epoch.

apparent in the opening sentence. It runs for sixteen lines before the poet can find a way to turn it off.[1]

The story takes an interesting turn when Satan climbs inside a sleeping serpent without waking him.[2] He just wants to borrow his skin as a disguise, while he tempts Eve. His plan works out, because Eve succumbs to his flattery, never having been cajoled by a snake before. She eats the Forbidden Fruit, which tastes all the better because it has been out of season, or out of bounds, twelve months in the year. From then on everything goes wrong. For instance Adam and Eve notice, to their embarrassment, that they are stark naked. Though they

[1] The poem is full of apostrophes, but what Milton needs is periods.

[2] He got in through the serpent's mouth, the serpent fortunately sleeping with his mouth open.

Unable to hide their guilt

put on some fig leaves, they are unable, as Milton says, to hide their guilt. In the end they are forced to leave Eden, the only home they have ever known. But, as Milton points out, trying to be cheerful about it, "The world was all before them," and they could go anywhere they wanted. The air was good. Lakes and streams were unpolluted. Land, though unimproved, was plentiful. It was not a bad time to be starting out.

When Milton said he was writing a sequel to *Paradise Lost*, readers eagerly looked forward to something on the order of *Satan Rides Again* or *Return of the Serpent*. *Paradise Regained* wasn't quite what they expected.

V

Seventeenth-Century Prose

MILTON, as we have seen, wrote prose with his left hand. This enabled him to say, when he had read a piece of prose by one of his right-handed contemporaries, "I could have written that with my left hand." Seventeenth-century prose, according to one critic, "is more like poetry than it has ever been since." What he means is that, like poetry, almost no one reads it. Many of the prose writers of this period were clergymen, supported by the church or the government, and there was no need for them to write anything good enough to sell.

Robert Burton

Robert Burton is said to have written *The Anatomy of Melancholy* to keep himself from going insane. "His mind was dark," says his biographer, having looked inside, probably through an ear, and been unable to see a thing.[1] Burton had another way of cheering

[1] Burton is said to have "spent his life in a bookcase." No wonder he was a little odd, as well as stiff.

himself up, besides reading and writing about melancholy. This was listening to bargemen swear. When he left them, with their curses ringing in his ears, he somehow felt better.

In his suggestion of cures for different kinds of melancholy, Burton sounds like a physician, though actually he was a clergyman. Had he been a surgeon, or a medical student, he might have written *The Melancholy of Anatomy*. Burton's proposed cures include diet, purges, bloodletting, and listening to music. One treatment he recommends is boring a hole in the skull to let out the fuliginous vapours, but he advises patients to go to a specialist,[1] and not try to do it themselves. Burton is particularly good on love-melancholy, which he thinks is mostly caused by women. He uses a number of four-letter words, such as "lust," but unfortunately some of the best passages are in Latin.

Sir Thomas Browne

Unlike Burton, a clergyman who wrote about medicine, Sir Thomas Browne was a doctor who wrote about religion. But he wrote on many other themes. His *Pseudodoxia Epidemica*, for instance, considers such matters as the habits of unicorns, earwigs, and glow worms, whether it is true that an elephant has no joints, and the musical note of the swan before its death. He was always writing about out-of-the-way subjects. When he finished one of these he said, "Well, that's out of the way." One of the things that fascinated him was the odd

[1] I.e., to the head man.

chance that a man might die on his birthday. As a matter of fact this happened to Browne himself, when he was seventy-seven, and it would be a pity if he never knew.[1]

Browne was too busy making a study of ancient funeral urns to realize there was a Civil War going on in England. Many thought him an eccentric, but he managed to stay out of the Army.[2]

His great work is *Religio Medici*, widely thought (by those who have not read it) to be about Religio, a relative of Lorenzo.

[1] Of course he may have planned it that way, sitting there with a calendar in one hand and a pistol in the other.

[2] Another project he was busy with, that also got him a deferment, was writing "A Dialogue Between Two Twins in the Womb Concerning the World They Were to Come Into." The twins had nine months to while away.

It is a good idea to keep an unabridged dictionary at hand while reading Sir Thomas Browne, unless you commonly use such words as indigitate, piaculous, ubiquitary, tapid, and transpeciate.

Taylor and Fuller

Two writers who can be taken up together are Jeremy Taylor and Thomas Fuller, both of them Royalists and preachers. Critics use superlatives when writing about Taylor, one of them calling him "the least read author of his time." Anyone interested in death will enjoy his *The Rule and Exercise of Holy Dying*.[1] The section called "Consideration of the miseries of man's life" leaves one filled with philosophical speculation, such as whether to shoot oneself, take poison, or slash both wrists. "We have gnats in our chambers and worms in our gardens and spiders and flies in the palaces of the greatest kings," writes Taylor, born three hundred years before the Age of Insecticides. He only wishes everyone could be as depressed as he is. To make a start, he urges his readers to go to a hospital and listen to the groans of the sick.

Thomas Fuller was somewhat more optimistic, one of his books being entitled *Good Thoughts in Bad Times*. Two years later, still keeping a stiff upper lip, he published *Good Thoughts in Worse Times*. When Cromwell came to power, we are told, "Fuller was allowed to

[1] A book that should be in the waiting room of every funeral parlor. Death as a way of getting exercise may not have occurred to you.

48

Taylor and Fuller

preach on sufferance," a subject that must have appealed to him.

The Holy State and the Profane State and *The Worthies of England* are full of anecdotes and witticisms, and it is not hard to keep from laughing out loud. Fuller had a remarkable memory. He told Pepys that he once dictated in Latin to four eminent scholars on four different subjects faster than they were able to write, until they were tired out.[1] In *The Holy State and the Profane State* he says the memory is lodged in the rear of the head, because that is where men scratch when they are at a loss. Of course they could stimulate their thinking better if only the skull weren't in the way.

[1] Luckily for Fuller, none of them knew shorthand.

Izaak Walton

Though Izaak Walton was also a biographer, he is best known for *The Compleat Angler* (often misspelled *The Complete Angler*).[1] This work takes the form of a discussion by an angler, a hunter, and a falconer during a fishing expedition. The three men talk steadily for five days, arguing, quoting poems, and frightening away the fish. Walton professes to like a quiet life, but only if he has no one to listen to him tell how to put a hook through a lob-worm or how to dress a chub.[2]

The Compleat Angler is full of fascinating lore. One chapter, for instance, is entitled "Observations of the Eel, and Other Fish that Want Scales." The observations of an eel, especially if you have never heard an eel's opinions on this and that, are certain to be interest-

[1] The original edition was illustrated with cuts of fish.
[2] Until it is caught, the chub goes around undressed. It is easier to swim that way.

ing. And you may not have realized how much the fish who do not have scales want them.

Sometimes Walton digresses a little. Amidst an explanation of how to fish for pike he gets off on frogs, the breeding habits of water-snakes, and a book by Dubravius, a bishop in Bohemia. "But whither am I going?" he asks. "I had almost lost myself." The reader sympathizes, having also been wandering around for several pages.

John Bunyan

John Bunyan was, by his own admission, very sinful as a young man. He was guilty of playing games and dancing, and even using swear words.[1] When he was nine or ten, he was the naughtiest boy in the block. Then everything changed. As he says in *Grace Abounding to the Chief of Sinners*,[2] "I began to look into the Bible with new eyes," perhaps meaning that he had got some stronger glasses. It was not easy to stop being a sinner. Dancing was probably the hardest to give up. It was a full year before he could kick the habit. Finally, though, he was saved, and having stopped doing everything that was fun was really happy. Never again would he write such a tract as *A Few Sighs from Hell, or the Groans of a Damned Soul.*

The title of Bunyan's *Pilgrim's Progress* confuses many persons who think that, with all that walking, it

[1] His father was a tinker, and he may have picked up a tinker's damn.

[2] The other boys referred to him as "Chief."

Hardest to give up

should be *Pilgrim's Bunyan*. At any rate it is a religious allegory, telling about Christian's journey from the City of Destruction to the Celestial City, by way of the Slough of Despond, the Valley of Humiliation, and other places that are all right to visit but you wouldn't want to live there. Persons who tire of the struggle to get across rivers should read the abridged version.

Bunyan wrote *Pilgrim's Progress* while he was in prison, serving a twelve-year term for preaching. Surely his sermons couldn't have been *that* bad.

Samuel Pepys

Samuel Pepys is the author of Pepys' *Diary*. The story of its discovery is fascinating. According to his biographer: "Pepys the man alive lay slumbering inside those closely written pages of his Diary until John Smith, a clergyman, working from 1819 to 1822, woke him up for us from his long sleep." Since he had been in

Samuel Pepys

there since 1669, when he stopped writing because of failing eyesight, it was a sleep of 153 years, or 133 years longer than Rip Van Winkle's nap. What is even more remarkable is the Rev. Smith's working over him for three years, no doubt using artificial respiration, slapping his cheeks, and pleading, "Snap out of it, Sam!" [1]

In the *Diary* Pepys tells all. He dwells on such intimate matters as sending his mother some tainted cheese, worrying over the fact that his wife's hair is falling out, and singing hymns in the morning before getting out of bed. As one critic has said, "He dilates on everything," though whether it is his eyes or his nostrils that dilate we do not know.

The most famous quotation from Pepys, who was something of an old roué, is "And so to bed." [2]

---

[1] According to another version, the book was written in code. The problem was to break the code without hurting Pepys.

[2] As he tells in his *Diary*, Pepys fined himself for every kiss over one that he stole from a pretty woman. Apparently the first one was free, and by moving around he could keep from owing himself too much.

VI

The Restoration

THE RESTORATION was not quite so spectacular as may at first be supposed. Charles I was not restored, or even revived. It was Charles II who assumed the throne. He had been in France, and when he came back to England he brought a large supply of snuff, perfumed handkerchiefs, fans, courtiers, and courtesans. The Puritans, who had been living simply and dressing plainly, were in for a ruff time of it.

The Puritans had kept the theaters closed, thinking them a hotbed of immorality.[1] The theatrical crowd, they felt, was full of bad actors. They looked askance [2] at actresses, and clutched their prayer books a little more tightly. Toward the end of the Puritan period, it is true, a play was now and then staged. But it was always called something like "An Allegorical Entertainment by Declamation and Music," and everyone pretended not to catch on.

With the Restoration, everything was out in the open, especially with actresses wearing low-cut dresses and being corseted in the middle. Wycherley's *Country*

[1] The very word "hotbed" made them blush.
[2] I.e., out of the corner of their eyes.

Wife was widely hailed by the critics as "coarse," "indecent," and "lecherous," and the theater was jammed. William Congreve is considered the greatest of the Restoration dramatists, perhaps because, as has been said, "He outstrips them all."

Congreve's *The Way of the World* is an excellent example of the Restoration comedy of manners.[1] The crux of the plot has been summed up as follows: "Mirabell is in love with Millamant, a niece of Lady Wishfort, and has pretended to make love to the aunt in order to conceal his suit of the niece." Toward the end of the play, after much deceit and intrigue, Lady Wishfort comes upon Mirabell pressing his suit. She consents to Mirabell's marriage to Millamant rather than have the play go on any longer.

The Way of the World may have been a failure, but it made a contribution to English drama by causing Congreve to quit writing for the stage.

John Dryden

According to one literary historian, "Dryden's dates are very suggestive to the student of English literature." They are 1631–1700, and what is suggestive about them is hard to see.[2] At any rate, few English authors have had the good fortune to be born in so auspicious a place as the vicarage of Aldwinkle All Saints, between Thrapston and Oundle.

[1] Bad manners, that is, these being funnier.
[2] Compare, for instance, 1631–1700 with 38-23-36.

56

Dryden's plays were mostly tragedies. Nevertheless he went on writing, undismayed. For some years he wrote his plays, such as *The Conquest of Granada*, in rhymed couplets. Then he suddenly shifted to blank verse, perhaps because he had misplaced his rhyming dictionary.

Dryden was a versatile writer, being able to write poems in praise of either Cromwell or King Charles II.[1] As a critic, he wrote *An Essay of Dramatic Poesy*, in the preface to which he mentions "The drift of the ensuing discourse." This prepares the reader for the fact that the *Essay* consists of a conversation by four men as they are seated in a barge, drifting down the Thames. As a satirist, Dryden wrote *Absalom and Achitophel*, about

[1] Pro-Puritan, pro-Royalist, and later pro-Catholic, he was a real pro.

None but the brave

Absalom (Monmouth), Achitophel (Shaftesbury), David (Charles II), and others (others).

As a poet, Dryden will long be remembered for the famous line which he approaches so hesitantly in *Alexander's Feast:*

> Happy, happy, happy pair!
>   None but the brave,
>   None but the brave,
> None but the brave deserves the fair.

We shall say nothing of his *Anus Mirabilis.*

VII

The Age of Pope

EIGHTEENTH-CENTURY literature having begun in 1688, it is difficult to find a name for this period. It has been called the Neo-Classical Age, the Augustan Age, the Age of Satire, the Skeptical Age, and the Age of Sense. The one thing all of these have in common is Age. Luckily, Pope was born in 1688, right on the nose, so the most popular name is the Age of Pope. When anyone asked him, in 1700, "What is your Age?" he came right back, "Twelve." Pope was small for his Age, but smart.

Because of mercantilism, foreign trade, and eating too much starch, this period saw the spread of the middle class. At this time also two political parties, the Whigs and the Tories, came into being. Henceforth people could be more specific about what it was they hated. Writers sat around in coffeehouses, referring to each other as "old bean" and sopping up local color.[1] Instead of writing romances set in distant lands, they wrote about everyday London. That is why there is so much emphasis on cheating, thievery, blackmail, and something referred to as whoring. Commonplace

[1] Especially when they spilled their coffee.

though these themes were, they were handled with wit.[1]

Daniel Defoe

Anyone who started out with a name like Foe, was the son of a butcher, and went to a school for Dissenters, was sure to have an interesting career. Changing his name to Defoe, probably to disguise his natural animosity, he did well in school in both Elementary and Advanced Dissent. His pamphlets against political and religious opponents reveal that he had learned much from watching his father at work with a cleaver. One of

[1] Many have tried to define wit, but no one has surpassed Dr. Johnson's famous definition, to wit: "Wit is wit."

Daniel Defoe

his pamphlets, *The Shortest Way with the Dissenters*, which suggests doing away with people who dissent, is full of irony. The supreme irony of it is that it was taken seriously and Defoe was fined, imprisoned, and exposed in the pillory.[1]

In his *The True-Born Englishman* are the famous lines:

> Wherever God erects a house of prayer,
> The Devil always builds a chapel there:
> And 'twill be found upon examination,
> The latter has the largest congregation.

If Defoe hoped these lines would be inscribed on the cornerstones of churches throughout the land, he was doomed to disappointment.

Defoe is said to have had a "genius for lying like truth." For instance in *A Journal of the Plague Year* he writes about the plague of 1665 as if he had been a grown man then, rather than a five-year-old boy. But instead of saying, "It's a lie," critics said, "What realism!" He continued lying in *Robinson Crusoe, Moll Flanders,* and other works and made such a success of it that other writers took it up. However they changed the name of it from lying to fiction. Somehow, prose fiction sounds better than prose lying.

Some think Defoe was the father of the modern novel. The story of Moll Flanders (who is seduced, unwittingly marries her own brother, becomes a success-

---

[1] Such is the hazard of writing with your tongue in your cheek instead of sticking it out so everyone will know how you really feel.

ful pickpocket and thief, and is deported from England with one of her former husbands, a highwayman) tends to bear this out.

Jonathan Swift

Jonathan Swift was a gloomy, ill-tempered man. He was plagued by misfortune, such as being born in Ireland. Also he had two women on his hands, Stella and Vanessa. It is not known whether he was secretly married to Stella, to whom he wrote his *Journal to Stella*, or even lived with her. But they were buried side by side, and in a church at that, without any eyebrows being raised.[1] What embittered Swift most was his being made only a dean, when he wanted to be a bishop.

[1] Some of *The Journal to Stella*, we might add, was written in what Swift calls his "little language," or baby talk. Take the passage: "Does MD never read at all now, pee? But oo walk plodigiousry, I suppose. . . . Nite deelest sollahs; farewell deelest Rives; rove poor Pdfr." Does oo understand?

Wanted to be a bishop

However he didn't realize how lucky he was, being made dean of a cathedral instead of a dean of men.

One of Swift's early works was *A Tale of a Tub*. It shows the genius of Swift by not being about a tub. It is about three brothers, each of whom is left a coat by their father. They are rather unusual coats, guaranteed to last for a lifetime and to grow along with the wearer.[1] The only catch is that no style changes are to be made in the coats. *A Tale of a Tub* is not only not about a tub, it is not about three brothers and their coats. It is about the Christian religion. If the reader is confused, he must remember that Swift hated people, and this is one way he had of getting back at them.

Swift's *A Modest Proposal* is easier to comprehend. Swift suggests that babies of the poor people of Ireland be fattened until they are a year old and then sold for meat. An American friend of his, who was something of a gourmet,[2] had told him how tasty such a child is, "whether stewed, roasted, baked, or boiled." Swift adds, showing his knowledge of cookery, "I make no doubt that it will equally serve in a fricassee or a ragout." Why Swift's proposal was not snapped up is hard to understand. Modest as it is, it is not only a practical solution of the population problem but full of mouth-watering recipes.

Swift's most popular work is *Gulliver's Travels*. Everyone knows about the Lilliputians and the Brobdingnagians, and everyone also knows how hard it is to

[1] Or, as Browning might have put it: "Grow big along with me."
[2] And a cannibal, of course. This was the average Englishman's idea of an American in those days, as it still is.

spell Houyhnhnm. Some feel that in referring to human beings as the "most pernicious race of little odious vermin that Nature ever suffered to crawl upon the face of the earth" Swift was overdoing it a little. But you can't please everyone.

Addison and Steele

Addison and Steele were forerunners of such literary partnerships as Gilbert and Sullivan and prove that two heads are almost as good as one good one. They were joint editors of the *Tatler* and the *Spectator*, which could be compared to modern newspapers except for their basic aim, which was to popularize morality and culture. They were intended to give people in the coffeehouses and chocolate houses [1] something to talk about, and prompted such spirited conversations as:

> "Have you read today's *Spectator?*"
> "Yes."

The two men are hard to tell apart. There were striking similarities, such as their being born in the same year. However Addison is said to be more "finished" as a writer, probably having reference to the fact that he finished writing earlier, dying ten years before Steele.

The writings of Addison and Steele mostly take the form of the familiar essay, with which everyone is familiar.

[1] Friendly places, even though, or perhaps because, a house is not a home.

Alexander Pope

Pope is said to "loom large" in English poetry, or perhaps he worked at a small loom, which made him look large by comparison. Actually he was only four feet six inches tall, which may be why some critics have never been able to see him as a poet.

Four feet six

As a boy, Pope seems to have been mathematically inclined. "I lisped in numbers, for the numbers came," Pope tells us in his *Epistle to Dr. Arbuthnot,* and we can hear the lad counting, "thixth, theven," and so on. But before long he turned to poetry and soon became famous. "His name was on every tongue," says one literary historian. Dentists and throat specialists must have been amazed.[1]

In *An Essay on Criticism* Pope sets down the rules for good writing. "A little learning is a dangerous thing," he says at one point, warning writers to think twice before fooling around with education. And later he urges:

> Be not the first by whom the new are tried,
> Nor yet the last to lay the old aside.

Those who have followed this advice, always checking on others before making a move, and taking pains to be neither ahead nor behind, have never quite got around to doing anything.[2]

The Rape of the Lock isn't as pornographic as the title would suggest. In an unusual twist, Belinda (Miss Arabella Fermor) isn't seriously harmed. It is a lock of hair that is ravished, or unlocked. The villain (Lord Petre) does it with his glittering forfex. This is what makes the poem a mock epic rather than the real thing. The action is quite different in *The Iliad*,[3] where Paris carries off all of Helen and not just a few strands of hair.

---

[1] Brain surgeons will appreciate Pope's "Most have the seeds of judgment in their mind." So that's what they are, they muse, poking around with their tweezers.

[2] By the way, it isn't necessary to have a volume of Pope's poetry if you wish to read *An Essay on Criticism*. Most of it is in Bartlett's *Familiar Quotations*.

[3] Which Pope translated, so he knew.

Pope's *Essay on Man* and his *Moral Essays* are written in heroic couplets.[1] Every two lines contain an Important Thought. For instance:

> Why has not Man a microscopic eye?
> For this plain reason, Man is not a Fly.

This may answer a question that has long troubled you. Think it over, when you are envious of a fly's ability to walk upside down on the ceiling. Can a fly play golf? Can a fly drive a car?

Pope insisted that "The proper study of mankind is man." He was proper to the last, though in his study of man he includes women.

---

[1] It was not Pope but another poet who said, "The Muse and I have been cohabiting, and we have had couplets."

VIII

The Early Novel

AS WE have noted earlier, some consider Defoe's *Robinson Crusoe* a novel. Others, however, call it a romance, though it is difficult to find much romance in the relationship between Robinson Crusoe and Friday. If *Robinson Crusoe* is not a novel, then the first English novels were those of Richardson. These at least have the prime requisite of the novel, indicated by such definitions as "a fictitious tale of considerable length" and "a long story." Richardson's novels are long, though not quite as long as they seem.

Samuel Richardson

Samuel Richardson was the son of a joiner, and pretty sociable himself. Even as a youth he wrote love letters for "illiterate sighing maidens," partly to be helpful and partly, no doubt, because he got in on some rather spicy affairs. It was not until he was fifty, however, that he published his first novel, *Pamela, or Virtue Rewarded*. It took four volumes for virtue to triumph.

Samuel Richardson

Pamela is written in the form of letters from a maid-servant named Pamela Andrews (actually Richardson, up to his old tricks). It was a great success, and immediately established Richardson as a man of letters. It tells how Pamela fights off the advances of a wicked, lecherous gentleman, Mr. B—, until finally he consents to marry her. Readers are on tenterhooks. "Will she or won't she?" they wonder. Men readers wonder whether she will give in to Mr. B—. Women readers wonder whether she will get Mr. B— to marry her. A few wonder what Mr. B—'s name is.

Richardson's greatest success was *Clarissa Harlowe*. In eight swift-moving [1] volumes it tells how Clarissa is drugged and raped by her dissolute lover, Robert Lovelace, how she dies in broken-hearted shame, and how Lovelace is stabbed in the end.[2] It is written in the form of letters from one character to another, and considering

[1] If you drop them from the window of a tall building.
[2] He made the mistake of turning his back.

how busy everyone is with chases, imprisonments, escapes, and whatnot, it is a wonder anyone has time to sign his name or lick a stamp. Clarissa's death is sad, until you remember she won't have to worry about that cad Lovelace any more.

Henry Fielding

"It would have been amusing to see Richardson and Henry Fielding side by side," writes a literary historian. "Two men could not have offered a sharper foil each to the other: the one a plump, stodgy, vain, middle-aged little man of business and novelist of sentiment; the other a burly youth of over six feet, strong and heavy, handsome, smiling, friendly, with patrician

Line-up

features, a glancing, humorous eye, and charm irresistable to man and woman alike."[1] It might have been amusing to see the two men side by side, as in a police line-up, but it is unlikely they would have stood there long, especially after Fielding's *Joseph Andrews*, making fun of Richardson's *Pamela*.

Fielding's most widely read work is *Tom Jones*. At the beginning of the novel Squire Allworthy finds a baby in his bed. Since the Squire is single, and it is a single bed, something is obviously amiss. It turns out that the baby is Tom Jones, a foundling. He is a pretty baby, and the Squire and his sister Bridget are always foundling him. Later Tom grows up and falls in love with Sophia Western and foundles her. However hundreds of pages and as many digressions separate Tom from the discovery that he is well born enough to marry Sophia, which he then does.[2] Fielding thoughtfully calms the impatient reader with his chapter headings, the last few of which are "Wherein the History Begins to Draw Toward a Conclusion," "The History Draws Nearer to a Conclusion," "Approaching Still Nearer to the End," and "In Which the History Is Concluded." It is a pity Richardson didn't do this in *Pamela* and *Clarissa Harlowe*. More readers might have been encouraged to read on to the End.

The most important thing about *Tom Jones* is the characters. As one critic says, "The immense canvas, when filled, contains forty figures." If you can visualize

[1] Can you guess which of the two novelists this critic preferred?

[2] Being born well and being well born are two different things.

a huge canvas bag stuffed with forty people, you will get some idea of Fielding's accomplishment.

Laurence Sterne

Laurence Sterne, we are told, was "sprung of good stock." Had he not been sprung, he might never have written *Tristram Shandy*. On the other hand, had he not suffered a sprained brain while being sprung he might not have written *Tristram Shandy* the way he did.

Though Sterne was a country parson, he was a cut-up and practical joker. "In full middle life," says his biographer, "he pulled off his wig and donned the cap and bells of Yorick." It must have been a startling scene, the way he yanked off that wig and grabbed Yorick's cap and bells. His wife went insane.[1]

Sterne had finished two volumes of *Tristram Shandy* and was trying it on some guests when several of them drowsed off. In a rage he threw the manuscript into the fire, but someone rescued it. By that time everyone was awake.

Tristram Shandy has been called "a richly stocked museum of queer and amusing bits of learning." One of the more amusing bits, also revealing Sterne's prose style, is the following: "My mother went down, and my father went on, reading the section as follows,

[1] "Sterne's ways were unpredictable," says one writer, "and his household was a constant jangle." The jangle, of course, came from the bells on his cap.

```
*    *    *    *    *    *    *    *    *
*    *    *    *    *    *    *    *    *
*    *    *    *    —Very well,—said my father,
*    *    *    *    *    *    *    *    *
*    *    *    *    *    *    *    *    *
*    *    *    *"
```

The end of *Tristram Shandy* comes not when Sterne has finished his story but when he has run out of dashes and asterisks.

IX

The Graveyard School

BRIEF mention should be made of a group of poets who belonged to the Graveyard School. They sat around happily in cemeteries, reading the inscriptions on tombstones, envying the dead, and hoping to see a ghost. Interested as they were in death, they loved the croaking of a crow. A newly opened grave was always a thrill, good for twenty or thirty lines of speculation about skulls, coffins, and worms.

Robert Blair

In *The Grave*, Robert Blair set a high standard for the Graveyard School. "The task be mine," he wrote, "to paint the gloomy horrors of the tomb." Actually he got more enjoyment out of it than he let on. His blood was always running chill, and this made him feel almost as good, on a warm summer night, as a cold drink. Here is a typical passage from *The Grave*:

Doors creak, and windows clap, and night's foul bird,
Rooked in the spire, screams loud.

Hoping to see a ghost

The windows seem to have shared Blair's enthusiasm, clapping that way. As for the poor bird, no wonder it screamed, the spire having rooked it. Perhaps the bird lit on the tip, which was sharper than it had suspected.[1]

Thomas Gray

Passing over Edward Young and his *Night Thoughts*, a poem said to "luxuriate in woe," we come to Thomas Gray.[2]

Gray was a small man. This may have been because of what has been called his "shrinking nature." He shrank from notoriety, he shrank from politics, he shrank from responsibility. One time he was sociable was when he went on the Grand Tour with Horace Walpole, but they had a falling out (luckily, not a falling off) in the Alps. One of the most scholarly of all English writers, he was appointed Professor of Modern History at Cambridge, but never delivered a lecture and therefore was never considered dull by the students.[3]

Gray was subject to fits of depression, during one of which he wrote his *Elegy Written in a Country Churchyard*. He had been poking around the cemetery at Stoke Poges, a place he could hardly wait to be buried in, when the idea for his poem came to him. A careful

[1] Blair was no intellectual, writing about "low-browed vaults."

[2] Unlike Walt Whitman, who was known as the good gray poet, he was known as the good poetic Gray.

[3] A full professorship with no teaching is the goal of most faculty members even today.

craftsman, he worked over the poem for seven years, which figures out almost exactly three weeks to a line. Sometimes he would take out a comma and then a few days later, after some hard thinking,[1] put it back in.

Everyone knows the first line of the *Elegy*:

The curfew tolls the knell of parting day,

though there are those who prefer it as it might have been quoted by the Rev. William A. Spooner:

The curfew knells the toll of darting pay.

The central theme of the poem seems to be that "The paths of glory lead but to the grave." In other words, everybody eventually dies. The thought is not original with Gray. It has long been recognized by morticians and by those who get up the statistics for insurance companies. But Gray, with his ten-syllable line, his chiseled phrases, and his personification, makes it sound better than "You gotta go sometime."

The *Elegy* won him Instant Fame.

[1] The word is "thinking," not "drinking."

X

The Age of Johnson

THE Age of Johnson was greater than the Age of Pope, Johnson living to seventy-five and Pope to fifty-six. This was a time when letter writing and conversation became fine arts. People like Horace Walpole and Mrs. Thrale and William Cowper kept postmen grumbling as they staggered under the load.[1] Letters were written, we are told, "with an eye to publication," though some used a quill pen for finer script. As for conversation, at any given time half the people of England were talking and the other half were taking down what they said. Occasionally those who listened said something too, such as "What was that again?" and "Wait till I get another bottle of ink."

Samuel Johnson

Samuel Johnson is usually called Dr. Johnson, either because of his honorary Doctor of Laws degree from

---

[1] In one edition there are over 3000 of Walpole's letters, written to 160 different persons. Walpole was a bachelor, probably unable to afford a wife because of all that postage.

Cambridge or because he was so much doctored for his many infirmities. He had a disease called king's evil, which was supposed to be cured when the patient was touched by a king.[1] When Johnson was three years old he was taken to Queen Anne, hoping the feminine touch would help, but it did no good.[2]

For many years Johnson was very poor. This gave him his chief motive for writing: money. One difference between Johnson and most writers is that he not only wrote for money but admitted it. "No one but a blockhead ever wrote except for money," he declared, and no one dared call Johnson a blockhead to his face. Since his income depended on his output, he wrote as fast as he could. He wrote forty-eight pages of his *Life of Savage* at one sitting, *The Vanity of Human Wishes* at the rate of a hundred lines a day, and *Rasselas* during the eve-

[1] No medical training was required.

[2] The Queen herself was touched when she saw poor little Sam, with his scrofula, convulsions, and only one good eye.

A good hater

nings of one week. He may not have been the best writer of the eighteenth century, but he was the fastest.

Johnson hated Americans, Scots, Irish, French, Italians, and Whigs. "He was a good hater," says one of his biographers admiringly. But he liked cats, which kept him from a perfect record.

Johnson's greatest project was his *Dictionary*, a definitive work. In view of his being the founder of the Literary Club in London, it is interesting to note his definition of Club: "An assembly of good fellows, meeting under certain conditions." What these conditions were, he did not say, but he may have had in mind such things as good liquor, good talk, and no women present, at least not wives. With publication of his *Dictionary*, Johnson became known as the Great Lexicographer. Those who don't know the meaning of lexicographer can look it up in Johnson's *Dictionary*.[1]

In his later years Johnson received a pension and was able to write less and talk more. It is interesting to conjecture about Johnson's literary career had he been paid for talking and not for writing instead of the other way around.

James Boswell

Boswell is described as having "a burning, steady eye." It must have been disconcerting to people the first time they saw him. He is also said to have had an eye for the ladies, though whether this was the burning one

[1] Johnson defines a lexicographer as "A writer of dictionaries, a harmless drudge," and he ought to know.

or the other one is not made clear. Boswell was a Scots-man. He told Johnson he was sorry about it but it couldn't be helped, and Johnson forgave him.

Boswell met Johnson when he was twenty-two and Johnson past fifty. At their first meeting, in the back parlor of Tom Davies' bookshop, Johnson was curt and rough, but this was just his way of showing how fond he was of someone. From then on, Boswell spent every

James
Boswell

minute he could in Johnson's company. It must have been the man's appearance that fascinated him. As Bos-well describes him on one occasion: "His brown suit of clothes looked very rusty; he had on a little old shriv-elled unpowdered wig, which was too small for his head; his shirt-neck and knees of his breeches were loose; his black worsted stockings ill drawn up; and he had a pair of unbuckled shoes by way of slippers." Boswell himself was a dandy, and he liked a man with a sense of style.

The way Boswell wrote his *Life of Johnson* was to listen to what Johnson said and then run to his rooms and write everything down before he forgot it. For a long time people thought Boswell spent every minute either listening to Johnson, running home, or writing. But with publication of his journals and private papers it was discovered he had other things on his mind, mostly women. A book that would make racier reading than Boswell's *Life of Johnson* would be Johnson's *Life of Boswell.*

Oliver Goldsmith

Just as Johnson is often called Dr. Johnson, Goldsmith is often called Dr. Goldsmith. He studied medicine for a time, but there is some suspicion that he never got an M.D. "I do not practice," he once said. "I make it a rule to prescribe only for my friends." "Pray, dear Doctor," his friend Beauclerk said, "alter your rule, and prescribe only for your enemies." After that witty remark, Beauclerk was well advised not to accept any potion offered by Goldsmith, unless Goldsmith took a swallow of it first.

Lacking patients, Goldsmith once prescribed something for himself, when he was very ill. The remedy aggravated the malady and Goldsmith died.[1]

[1] Had he lingered on, he could have sued himself for malpractice.

O. Goldsmith

Goldsmith wrote essays, poems, plays, and a novel. His best-known poem is *The Deserted Village*. In the dedication to Sir Joshua Reynolds he says, "The only dedication I ever made was to my brother. . . . He is since dead. Permit me to inscribe this poem to you." The dedication seems not to have had the same tragic effect on Reynolds, who lived another twenty-two years.

In *The Deserted Village* Goldsmith yearns for the Good Old Days of simple living. Goldsmith was writing in 1770, and knew nothing of freeways, parking problems, smog, and the population explosion.[1] Nor had he ever seen a television commercial about perspiration odor, bad breath, or loose dentures. Had Goldsmith been able to look ahead as clearly as he could look

[1] In *The Deserted Village* he worries about underpopulation.

back, he would have bought up some real estate in Auburn and held it for his grandchildren.

The Vicar of Wakefield, concerning the misfortune and eventual triumph of the Rev. Dr. Primrose and his family, is said to have the most implausible plot of any novel in the eighteenth century.[1] It also includes the tender lyric beginning "When lovely woman stoops to folly." [2] Goldsmith makes a helpful suggestion to any woman who is foolish enough to let herself be betrayed by a man. The thing to do, Goldsmith says, is to die. That will teach him.[3]

---

[1] *Tristram Shandy* is not in competition, since it has no plot at all.

[2] The next line is not, but might well be, "In low-cut gown, men murmur, 'Golly!'"

[3] It will "wring his bosom," as Goldsmith puts it poetically. Goldsmith was a phrasemaker, though here "chest" would seem more appropriate than "bosom."

XI

The Pre-Romantics

CHANGE was in the air," says one literary historian, and we have a vision of shillings and pence being tossed about willy-nilly. Toward the end of the eighteenth century a new kind of poetry appeared, and with it a new kind of poet. Cowper had attacks of insanity, Macpherson was a forger, Burns drank too much, Blake had weird visions, and Chatterton committed suicide. These are the Pre-Romantics, preparing us for the incest, wife desertion, and drug addiction of the Great Romantics. Let us look at two of the most interesting writers of this period.

Robert Burns

Robert Burns [1] is considered a national hero in Scotland. He is admired for having worked his way up from poverty in the country to poverty in the city. Few men, even in Scotland, could drink so much and yet stay on their feet. And then there was his truly remarkable accomplishment of having illegitimate children by at least

[1] Originally Burnes or Burness. Some people don't know this.

five women.[1] He finally married Jean Armour, but not until she had had four children by him (two sets of twins) and was getting pretty insistent.

As a boy on his father's farm he read poetry while ploughing, and it is no wonder he had some of the crookedest furrows in Ayrshire. Later he was fortunate in obtaining a job with the excise service to help support his family. He was doubly fortunate in that this involved measuring beer barrels, a type of work he found congenial.

Burns could write in standard English, but he wrote best in his own Scottish dialect. Note, for instance, the line "Upon a simmer Sunday morn," in which "simmer" means "summer" but also gives the impression of

[1] Elizabeth Patton (or Paton), Mary Campbell, Jenny Clow, Jean Armour, and Anne Parker. There may have been others. Burns kept no very accurate records.

Congenial work

heat. Moreover, by using "a' " for "all," "an' " for "and," "sel' " for self," and so on he saved no telling how many letters. Lines that are completely incomprehensible, such as "Wha kent fu' weel to cleek the sterling" and "An' while I kittle hair on thairms," [1] at least have a nice lilt to them and can be set to music. No one expects to understand something being sung, anyhow.[2]

Many of Burns's poems have to do with his heart, which gave him a good deal of trouble. For instance there is "My heart is a-breaking, dear tittie," [3] and his famous

My heart's in the Highlands, my heart is not here;
My heart's in the Highlands, a-chasing the deer.

Burns, who was then in the Lowlands, must have had difficulty keeping up his blood pressure. But this is nothing compared with how terrified the deer must have been if it looked back over its shoulder.

Several of Burns's tenderest poems are addressed to Mary Campbell, whom he calls "bonie Mary" but seems to have loved anyhow. Other poems are to dogs, mice, daisies, and similar objects of his affection.

Burns's scariest poem is *Tam o' Shanter*. This describes the gruesome things Tam sees when he peeks into the auld haunted kirk, such as the bones of a murderer, five bloody tomahawks, and a garter that had strangled a baby when it was mistakenly put around its neck instead of its leg. The poem is subtitled "A Tale,"

[1] Which we are told has nothing to do with hair on the arms.

[2] Burns himself had no voice and couldn't carry a tune. But he could whistle, especially when the girls went by.

[3] Whatever you think, "tittie" means "sister."

perhaps because of what happens to poor Maggie, Tom's horse, just as it crosses the keystone of the bridge.

William Blake

All are agreed that William Blake was no ordinary man. As a boy he saw angels walking around in the hayfields, and one day he looked up and there was God peering at him through the window! He was never lonesome, because the spirits of great men of the past were always dropping in on him.

Blake had an advantage over most poets. He illustrated and printed his own poems, thus cutting out printers, artists, and publishers. He even made his own plates.[1] According to his biographer, "He always had a burin in his hand." When you realize that a burin is an engraver's tool, a sharp-pointed instrument, you will understand why some people kept their distance, especially those who thought him insane.

The poems in his *Songs of Innocence* are easy enough to comprehend. For instance there are his lines to a sick rose, beginning, "O Rose, thou art sick!" The rose is in a bad way, and should be transplanted from the flower bed to its deathbed. Sometimes, to be absolutely sure his meaning is clear, Blake repeats a difficult line, as in

> Little Lamb, I'll tell thee,
> Little Lamb, I'll tell thee.

[1] But not his cups and saucers.

But the reader may be a little uncertain about the meaning of poems such as *Jerusalem* and *The Book of Thel*. If so, he will be grateful to the critic who explains these works by calling them "roseate and cerulian fancies on a gossamer texture woven out of the songs of Shakespeare and the echoes of Fingal's airy hall."

Blake is said to have died with a smile on his face. He may have been thinking about some of the interpretations of his poems.

Never lonesome

XII

The Romantic Period

THE Romantic Period was a time of "flights of fancy," "wings of imagination," "emotional transport," and other new means of travel. Everyone wanted to get back to nature, including many who had never been there. There was widespread interest in man in his natural state.[1] The noble savage was greatly admired, and

[1] This interest is still alive today in nudist colonies.

Greatly admired

many people went to remote places to seek him out and get his opinion on current social and political problems. Some travelers failed to return, having run into ignoble savages by mistake.

William Wordsworth

The greatest of the Romantic poets was William Wordsworth. His greatness is indicated by his ability to write, in *The Prelude,* nearly 8000 lines about the growth of his mind.[1] While others were bird watchers, Wordsworth was a mind watcher, identifying every strange new thought and jotting down a description in his notebook.

He also liked to roam in the woods and look at Nature. "He lost his mother," we are told, perhaps because she wandered off from him and was not so familiar with the trails as he. His sister Dorothy, however, he was unable to lose, hard as he tried.[2] She kept a journal, and knew where she had been and what was going on.[3]

Wordsworth's best friend was Coleridge, with whom he collaborated on the *Lyrical Ballads.* Coleridge could walk almost as many days without stopping as Wordsworth. They both had good feet.[4] Wordsworth put up

[1] At that, it was just the beginning of a much longer poem Wordsworth was unable to finish, since he lived to be only eighty.

[2] "She remained unshaken," says Wordsworth's biographer.

[3] Dorothy lived with William even after he married. He knew she knew he had an illegitimate daughter in France, and if he threw her out she might publish her journal.

[4] Their feet were iambic, with a tendency to become anapestic after a hard day.

with Coleridge's incessant talking because he always hoped he would divorce his wife and marry Dorothy and take her away somewhere.

As he tells us in the Preface to the *Lyrical Ballads*, Wordsworth believed in using "language really used by men." He therefore listened intently to idiot boys, beggars, old leech gatherers, and others whom he met while working out at the Wye. This accounts for such powerful lines as "And then an open field they crossed" and "Right glad was he when he beheld her."

A lake poet

A lake poet, Wordsworth had water on his mind, writing much about rivers, ponds, and streams. Flowers such as daffodils and daisies troubled him deeply, perhaps because of the pollen. He had a way of talking to daisies ("Daisy! again I talk to thee"), and people who saw him down on his knees, in an animated conversation, tapped their heads or pretended not to notice.[1] He also believed that flowers enjoy the air they breathe, and claimed he could hear them inhale and exhale. It is because of their love of fresh air, he maintained, that flowers stay outdoors so much.

Wordsworth wrote several poems about Lucy. No one knows who Lucy was, and the clearest description we have is that she looked something like a violet by a mossy stone. Anyhow, this gives us an opportunity to correct the last stanza of one of the Lucy poems, *She Dwelt Among the Untrodden Ways*, and make it available in what was probably the original version:

> She lived unknown, and few could know
> When Lucy ceased to stir;
> But she is in her grave, and, oh,
> The difference to her!

Samuel Taylor Coleridge

Coleridge has been described as having "thick lips and an open mouth, since he could not breathe through his nose."[2] On the other hand his forehead was high and impressive, and Dorothy Wordsworth said he had a fine frenzy. Some of his contemporaries thought he was a misfit, but this may be because he wore suits that were a trifle too large.[3]

"He wrote only when the Muse called him," writes

[1] It was embarrassing to be introduced to a flower that just kept nodding.

[2] Nor could he talk with his mouth closed.

[3] See his experiment with pantisocracy.

one biographer. This probably explains why his best writing was done before he was thirty, since his hearing declined as he grew older. Then too, he was always stopping work for an opium break. One of his greatest problems was getting a prescription for drugs not sold over the counter, but he solved this by moving in with a physician. He had only dropped in for a little laudanum, but stayed eighteen years.[1]

Coleridge wrote poetry and prose, literary criticism and drama. His dramatic writings were probably his least successful, and it is no wonder he called one of his plays *Remorse*.

Coleridge, we are told, was "always the dreamer." Often his dreams showed the influence of laudanum or of something he had eaten just before going to bed. Once he had a dream about composing a poem, *Kubla Khan*, and when he awakened he started to write it down. But just as he was getting to the good part, about a damsel with a dulcimer, he was interrupted by a man who called on business. Coleridge does not say what business this person came on, but since he stayed more than an hour he must have been selling insurance or encyclopedias or demonstrating a vacuum cleaner. Anyhow, when he left, Coleridge was unable to remember the rest of his poem. He was always hoping to have the same dream again, and the next time he swore he wouldn't answer the doorbell.

The Rime of the Ancient Mariner is more of a nightmare. It is about an Ancient Mariner who stops a wed-

[1] Living with a physician also enabled Coleridge to get away from his wife. She came to see him a few times but gave up when she found she had to pay for an office call.

ding guest to tell him his strange story. Meanwhile the bride, who is waiting for all the guests to arrive, is about to explode. "Red as a rose is she," Coleridge says. The Ancient Mariner's story has an important moral: Never shoot an albatross that is harmlessly hanging around. The next thing you know it will be hanging around your neck.

Christabel is Coleridge's most medieval poem. Notice the medievalism of such a line as

Tu — whit! —— Tu — whoo!

Coleridge spent a year in Germany and is blamed for bringing German philosophy and literature to England. It would have been better, many think, if he had brought home beer steins, wood carvings, and cuckoo clocks like everyone else.

Sir Walter Scott

One of the most intriguing incidents in Scott's life is barely mentioned by his biographer. "A disappointment in love left a lifelong scar," this writer says.[1] We can only imagine the scene: a spunky Scottish lass pulling a knife on young Walter and almost finishing him off before friends could separate the pair. In later life Scott shrugged off the scar as an appendectomy.

Scott loved anything old. He built his home, Abbotsford, in the architecture of a medieval castle, something that would be frowned upon in the housing develop-

[1] Through a typographical error, this originally came out as "a lifelong scare." I have corrected it with some reluctance.

ments of today. He also loved the supernatural, and was delighted when his home became old enough that the doors began to squeak. On windy, rainy nights he would lie in bed and listen to the ghosts of Scottish heroes as they seeped around in their ectoplasm.

Scott became famous with *The Lay of the Last Minstrel*.[1] This is a narrative poem of old Scotland, "put in the mouth of an ancient minstrel," perhaps to keep him quiet. The meter is unusual, giving one the feeling of riding a horse at a brisk canto. Scott followed this with *The Lady of the Lake*, which is also full of love and heroism but has an important addition, a signet ring which on being presented to the king will make him grant a boon, an early instance of boondoggling.

Most loved of Scott's poems is *Lochinvar*. It tells of how Lochinvar came out of the west and snatched up the fair Ellen just as she was about to marry another, a laggard in love and a dastard in war.[2] Seldom has there been such a horseman as Lochinvar, though the "he" in

He staid not for brake, and he stopped not for stone,

must surely refer not to Lochinvar, who was none too staid, but to his horse. Lochinvar tugged on the brake and shouted, "Stop for that stone!" but the horse galloped on. An interesting incident in the poem is where Ellen kisses the goblet instead of Lochinvar. She should have worn her glasses, no matter how she looked in

[1] A careful reading of the poem fails to disclose what it was the minstrel laid.

[2] Her father's choice, not hers.

Sir Walter Scott

them. At the end of the poem Lochinvar carries off Ellen, and is last seen riding into the sunset, setting (or sunsetting) an example for countless films later produced in Hollywood.[1]

Scott also wrote thirty-two novels.

Anyone who wishes to know a little more about Scott can read the seven-volume biography by Lockhart, his son-in-law. It has been said that this "paints Scott at full length." We do not know at which end Lockhart started or what color he used. But when Scott was about to go outdoors, on a cold day, Lockhart said, "Wait till I put on another coat."

[1] He had come out of the west, in this early Western, and now was heading home.

Roasting a pig

Charles Lamb

Charles Lamb was apparently a sickly youth, since he went to school at Christ's Hospital. Later he was put away for a while in a madhouse. He was not really insane, but people got the idea he was from some of his puns.[1] His sister Mary, however, was more of a problem. "In a sudden fit of insanity," we are told, "she killed her mother with a knife as they were about to sit down at dinner, wounded her father, and only by Charles's interference was saved from further mischief." If not insane, she was mischievous. Of course she may only have been showing her displeasure at what they were going to have for dinner. It was her way of saying, "You *know* I don't like that" or "What, *again?*" Charles and Mary lived together most of their lives and were in the habit of taking long walks, especially when Mary had to trudge back to the asylum for a checkup.

Though Charles Lamb is best known for his essays, he also wrote poetry and a couple of plays. One of the latter, a comedy called *Mr. H—*, was "hissed off the stage," actors holding onto their hats, and scenery being blown every which way.

Lamb wrote his essays under the name of Elia, which is why they are called *The Essays of Elia*. One of his essays is *A Dissertation Upon Roast Pig*, explaining how to roast a pig and burn down your house at the same time. The main thing is to lock all the doors so the pig can't get out. Pigs don't like it, and neither do fire

[1] The author of the present volume has himself been getting some curious looks.

insurance companies. But as Lamb says, in his simple, informal way, "Of all the delicacies in the whole *mundus edibilis*, I will maintain it to be the most delicate—*princeps obsoniorum.*"

It has been said that Lamb loved old books, old wine, tobacco, whist, and punch brewed by his sister. Remembering the incident of his sister and the knife, he always had her drink a glass of the punch first.[1]

William Hazlitt

One of Lamb's circle was William Hazlitt, but unlike Lamb, who had mostly friends, Hazlitt had mostly enemies. "He stood alone," it has been said, unless he had had a little too much to drink. An example of what some called his fiercely independent spirit and others called his contrariness was his being for France when England was at war with that country. Yet in a letter to Leigh Hunt he said, "I want to know why everybody has such a dislike to me." Since almost no one was speaking to him, he had no way of finding out.

Hazlitt was deeply interested in art, philosophy, politics, and women. He had an affair with his landlady's daughter, probably thinking this went with the rent, and told all about it in *Liber Amoris*, or free love. Yet he could be shy and reticent. In *My First Acquaintance with Poets*, about his meeting with Coleridge, he begins: "My father was a Dissenting Minister at W-m in Shropshire." Most writers would have told the name of

[1] But she usually beat him to the punch anyhow.

the town, which was Wem, but Hazlitt held back. People thought it must surely be a vowel he left out, as in "d-mn," and guessed Wam, Wim, Wom, and Wum before they got it right.

A characteristic essay is his *On Going a Journey*. "I like to go by myself," he says, which is very different from Sterne's "Let me have a companion of my way." Hazlitt's reason for traveling alone is well put when he says, "I never quarrel with myself." [1] And what did Hazlitt do when he was on a journey? "I wish to vegetate," he explains, conjuring up a picture of this essayist standing in some distant garden, his feet dug into the soil, at the end of a row of beans.

Let us leave him there.

Thomas De Quincey

Like Coleridge, De Quincey became addicted to opium. Accounts differ on what started him on the habit. Some say he first took opium for a toothache, others say it was for dyspepsia, and still others say neuralgia. "Take two opium tablets," a doctor probably said in those days, instead of "Take two aspirin." Anyhow, De Quincey seems to have worked up to a larger dosage than Coleridge, eventually taking 8000 drops of laudanum a day. [2] As the title of *Confessions of an English Opium Eater* indicates, it was English opium he ate, since he was unable to afford the imported variety.

[1] Sometimes, however, his food disagreed with him.
[2] Just counting the 8000 drops was a full-time job.

De Quincey wrote ornate, impassioned prose, which he referred to as "the literature of power." It is more evident in *On Murder as One of the Fine Arts* than in *The Logic of Political Economy*, perhaps because De Quincey's heart was really more in murder.

Despite the opium habit and his preoccupation with sudden death,[1] De Quincey lived to be seventy-four. This may be attributed to his habit of deep breathing, described in *Sighs from the Depths*.

[1] See his *The Vision of Sudden Death* and *Dream Fugue on the Theme of Sudden Death*. It is a pity De Quincey lived before the era of the motor car.

Ate only British opium

George Gordon, Lord Byron

Let us make clear at the outset that George Gordon and Lord Byron are the same person, though he did so much in his short life that some think he must surely have been two people, or even three. Byron himself said that a man's life should be measured not by his years but by his experiences, and on this basis he was a senior citizen by the time he was twenty.[1]

Byron had an unusual family background. His father was a rake. His grandfather, an admiral in the Navy, was called "Foul Weather Jack" by his men but "Foul Language Jack" by those unaccustomed to the way sailors talk. His mother was an erratic woman who "alternately petted and abused her only child," and Byron tried to keep out of sight on alternate days. It is no wonder Byron blamed his ancestry when he got out of line a little. "I can't help it," he said, after a night of debauchery. By having a daughter by his half-sister, Augusta,[2] he hoped to confuse the genealogists.[3]

When he was at Cambridge, Byron seems not to have studied any too hard, being busy with cricket, swimming, boxing, and wild parties. While he was still a student, he published a book called *Hours of Idleness*

[1] At his birthday party it was always hard to know how many candles to put on the cake.

[2] This is believed only by those who like to think the worst. In other words, most.

[3] Byron also had a child by Claire Clairmont, Shelley's wife's stepsister. Byron had relations all over. See especially the Countess Guiccioli, with whom he lived in Venice, Pisa, Ravenna, and Genoa. It was a moving experience.

that was savagely attacked by literary critics and university authorities. Before long he was in Europe, traveling under the pseudonym of Childe Harold and establishing himself as a writer by swimming the Hellespont. When he published the first two cantos of *Childe Harold's Pilgrimage*, he awoke to find himself still tired.

The last eight years of his life Byron spent as an exile, traveling about from woman to woman. One of his most beautiful lyrics, *Maid of Athens, Ere We Part*,

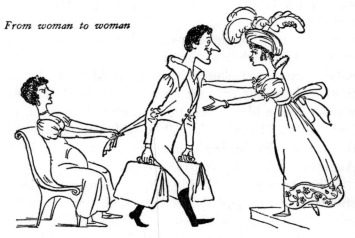

From woman to woman

he wrote after falling in love with his landlady's daughter.[1] He left in a hurry, flying to Istambol. Before leaving, he asked the girl to give him back his heart, which she had been keeping for him, or, if she wouldn't do that, to take the rest of him. He wanted to keep everything together. No mere lip presser, Byron got more out of kissing than most men. "By that lip I long to

[1] See Hazlitt, above. A landlady with an attractive young daughter should think twice before renting a room to a writer.

taste," he says, showing he bit a bit.[1]

Another beautiful lyric is his *So We'll Go No More A-Roving*. With a slight emendation, to bring it up to date, one stanza goes:

> For the sword outwears its sheath,
>   And the soul wears out the breast,
>   And the pants go, underneath,
>   And all that's left is vest.

Byron is said to have written *The Prisoner of Chillon* on two rainy days. This may explain the Gothic mould that had begun to form on the seven pillars. As for *Childe Harold's Pilgrimage*, Childe Harold is no childe, or at any rate is old enough to have run through Sin's long labyrinth, which must have taken a little time. Byron has trouble keeping track of his hero. "But where is Harold?" he asks at one point. If Byron doesn't know, how can he expect his reader to?

One of Byron's specialties is saying "Hail!"[2] For instance there is his beautiful "Hail, Muse! *et cetera*" in *Don Juan*. He is also good at "Farewell!" In the final stanza of *Childe Harold* he says "Farewell!" three times before signing off.

It is appropriate that we leave Byron with a hail and farewell.

---

[1] See also *To Caroline*, thought to refer to Lady Caroline Lamb, where Byron says, "For e'en your lip seems steep'd in snow." Not only taste but temperature goes into a good kiss. And in *Don Juan* Byron mentions still another requisite:
> for a kiss's strength,
> I think, it must be reckoned by its length.

[2] Byron was a great one for proposing a toast to almost anything, especially when drinking out of a skull and using a small, slender bone as a swizzle stick.

Percy Bysshe Shelley

Shelley was such a firm believer in freedom, justice, equality, and the brotherhood of man that he was thought unbalanced. In school he was known as "Mad Shelley."

For a Romantic poet, his life was relatively uneventful. He was expelled from Oxford,[1] eloped with the sixteen-year-old daughter of an innkeeper, left her to drown herself, ran off with another woman, traveled around with Byron, preached the overthrow of established governments and their replacement by anarchy, and was drowned shortly before his thirtieth birthday.

[1] He had done nothing but publish a pamphlet called "The Necessity of Atheism."

Percy B. Shelley

As for the woman he ran off with, she was the daughter of a man who advocated free love (except when it involved his daughter). She was also the author of *Frankenstein*, which shows what she must have been thinking about during those long silences.

Shelley, we are told, "was always yearning for the unattainable." An example of this is in his *Ode to the West Wind*, when he wishes he were a dead leaf. This seems a modest enough ambition, but Shelley never made it. More puzzling, in view of his staunch support of truth, is his request in the same poem to be a lyre. He also had a way of identifying himself with things. In *The Cloud* he is a cloud, though he seems also to be a bird, shaking the dew from his wings, and at another point a sailing ship with a rather unusual passenger, the sunrise. Shelley must have been an interesting person to invite to a masquerade party, with everyone wondering, "What do you suppose Percy will come as tonight?"

Everything, to Shelley, was like something else, and he could never quite make up his mind what. Thus in *To a Skylark* a skylark is like a cloud of fire, like an unbodied joy,[1] like a star, like a poet, like a high-born maiden, like a glowworm, and like a rose. In *Hymn to Intellectual Beauty* intellectual beauty is like moonbeams, like hues and harmonies of evening, like clouds, like memory of music, and so on. Without the word "like," Shelley would have been helpless.

In *Adonais*, his poem about Keats, Shelley contradicts himself. In the opening line he says, "I weep for Adonais—he is dead!" But toward the end of the poem

[1] This may be a little hard for you to picture.

he says, "Peace, peace! he is not dead!" If he changed his mind, he should have gone back and revised the first part of the poem. Or if he was unsure, he could have asked some of Keats's friends or checked at the Public Records Office.

Shelley's most ambitious work is a lyrical drama, *Prometheus Unbound*. Prometheus is being punished by Jupiter for giving fire to man, and in view of such subsequent developments as arson and overcooked food, Jupiter appears to have been justified. At the beginning of the first act, Prometheus is bound to a precipice and has had no sleep for three thousand years.[1] Eventually Prometheus is freed by Hercules, and we hear nothing more of him in the last act. Probably he is catching up on all that lost sleep.

When Shelley's boat capsized, he is said to have had a volume of Sophocles in one pocket and a volume of Keats in the other. Had these not dragged him down, he might have made it to shore.

John Keats

John Keats had consumption. This kept him from marrying Fanny Brawne, who was afraid of germs. When he died and was buried in Rome, Fanny's letters were buried with him.[2]

One of Keats's biographers is Amy Lowell, the American poet who smoked cigars. Her biography is

---

[1] He may be bound, but his patience is boundless.

[2] The original dead letter office. Keats's own signature was hard to make out. His name was writ in water.

Loved everything Greek

longer than Keats's *Complete Poems*. Opposite the title page is a picture of the mask Keats wore all his life.

Keats loved everything Greek. An example is the Elgin marbles, which he could imagine boys playing with in ancient Athens. However when he first saw them, as he writes in *On Seeing the Elgin Marbles for the First Time*, the emotional impact must have been too much for him, because he felt like a sick eagle.[1] One of his most Greek works is *Endymion*.[2] This is about a love affair between Endymion, a shepherd boy, and Cynthia, the moon goddess. Endymion was aiming pretty high. It contains the great Hymn to Pan, which was panned by most of the critics, and such lines as

> And now, as deep into the wood as we
> Might mark a lynx's eye.

How to get a lynx to stand still long enough for you to mark its eye is something Keats does not explain. One of Endymion's difficulties, as a lover, is that he is always going to sleep. His dreams, however, are almost as good as the real thing.[3]

Not only in the dreams of Endymion but in many other poems Keats is preoccupied with sleep. He was lucky not to have gone sleepless for three thousand years, like Prometheus. Notice, for example, *Sleep and Poetry* and his sonnet *To Sleep*, the latter describing

[1] An interesting simile. It is better to be a sick eagle than to be walking beneath one.

[2] "It's Greek to me," students have said for years.

[3] Describing one of Endymion's dreams of kissing, Keats refers to "Those lips, O slippery blisses." Endymion seems to have had trouble getting traction.

somewhat gruesomely how sleep turns the key that locks "the hushed casket of my soul." In the same poem sleep is a "soft embalmer," and one gains the impression that it could run a mortuary almost single handed. In *Ode to a Nightingale,* however, Keats becomes a bit confused. "Do I wake or sleep?" he asks. You sympathize with him and his need to know.

We shall conclude our treatment of Keats and the Romantic Poets with those oft-quoted lines from his *Ode to a Grecian Urn:*

> Heard melodies are sweet, but those unheard
> Are sweeter.

As students are always helpfully pointing out, Keats means it is nice to listen to music but nicer not to.

XIII

The Victorian Era

ACCORDING to one historian, "The period of sentiment and self-indulgence ended when Victoria came to the throne. The English people became high-minded, modest, self-righteous, and enterprising." Naturally, this sudden change affected writers. It is hard to imagine Tennyson having an illegitimate child, like Wordsworth, or Browning leaving his wife to run off with another woman, like Shelley,[1] or Thomas Babington Macaulay getting hooked on opium, like Coleridge. They were too afraid of what Queen Victoria might say, perhaps something devastating, such as "We are not amused."

With the repeal of the Corn Laws, there was nothing to prevent Victorian literature.

Thomas Carlyle

Thomas Carlyle's belief in hard work is perhaps traceable to his birthplace, Ecclefechan, which is about

---

[1] Or, in that event, Elizabeth Barrett Browning throwing herself into the river. She didn't have the strength to throw a stone.

Loved hard work

as hard to spell and to pronounce as the birthplace of any English author.[1] When he was fourteen years old he walked ninety miles to enter the University of Edinburgh. How he got into the university when he was so young is not known. Perhaps the Director of Admissions asked him how old he was and Carlyle replied, "Ninety," thinking of the miles he had walked.

Carlyle had a Scotch burr, probably picked up while walking through the fields. With this burr and a bad case of stomach trouble, it is no wonder he was crotchety and irritable. One of the few people who could get along with him was Emerson, who also believed in independence, hard work, and being opinionated. Like Coleridge, Carlyle was influenced by German writers, such as Sturm and Drang, and in *Sartor Resartus* occasionally translates an English word or phrase into German to help the reader.[2]

In *Sartor Resartus* Carlyle writes about clothes, and his style is suitable. Probably no English writer has relied so heavily on the comma. A typical sentence begins: "To such readers as have reflected, what can be called reflecting, on man's life, and happily discovered, in contradiction to my Profit-and-Loss Philosophy, speculative and practical, that. . . ." Some say that after his wife died Carlyle was in a comma the rest of his life.

Carlyle's idea about clothes is that what is really important is underneath. It was embarrassing to be out with Carlyle, sometimes known as Peeping Tom, as he looked for the Everlasting Yea.

[1] Being born in Ecclefechan he couldn't help, but Craigenputtock, where he later lived, was his own choice.

[2] The German reader, that is.

In *Heroes and Hero Worship* and *The French Revolution* Carlyle shows that men make history, or at least history books. The most interesting thing about *The French Revolution* is Carlyle's lending his only copy of the manuscript of the first volume to his friend John Stuart Mill, whose servant used it to start a fire.[1] Carlyle had already destroyed his notes (he had a fire to start too), and had to begin all over. As he slaved away, trying to remember what he wrote the first time, Carlyle kept saying over and over to himself: "There is a perennial nobleness, and even sacredness, in Work."

Alfred, Lord Tennyson

Though some may have thought Tennyson reserved, it is said he was "an excellent companion with intimates, breaking at times into heroic laughter." His friends were always telling him funny stories, just to hear that laugh of his.[2]

In 1832 Tennyson published a volume called *Poems,* which got bad reviews. After publishing nothing for ten years, he brought out another book called *Poems.* This was highly praised, proving it was not the title of the earlier work that was at fault. The books came out rapidly thereafter. Despite the fact that some of his poems are called idylls, Tennyson was a hard worker.

One of Tennyson's most memorable poems is *The*

[1] In the fireplace. The incident was bad enough without involving arson. J. S. Mill, by the way, said he was sorry.

[2] However in Cambridge he belonged to a group known as the Apostles "because of their moral earnestness." When he was with them, Tennyson tried not to laugh too uproariously.

Lady of Shalott. What makes it so memorable, and so easily memorized, is that Tennyson says "The Lady of Shalott" thirteen times in the poem. Very rarely does anyone ask, "What is the name of that poem about the Lady of Shalott?" Another well-known poem is *Locksley Hall,* especially the line, "In the spring a young man's fancy lightly turns to thoughts of love." [1] For some reason, this line is better known than the line rhyming with it, "In the spring a livelier iris changes on the burnished dove."

In Memoriam, it is said, "contains many run-over lines," but we do not know what ran over them. The poem expresses Tennyson's grief at the death of his friend Arthur Hallam, who was engaged to Tennyson's sister. Arthur and the girl had looked forward to a long, happy engagement, perhaps like Tennyson's, that lasted almost fourteen years.

[1] Another version of this is "In the spring a young man's fancy, but a young woman's fancier."

Alfred Lord Tennyson

As for Tennyson's *Idylls of the King,* some critics feel that King Arthur resembles Queen Victoria's husband, Prince Albert. If so, this did not stand in the way of Tennyson's appointment as Poet Laureate.

Lovers of poetry are grateful to Tennyson. They are grateful that he did not write all of his poems in the dialect he uses in his *Northern Farmer, Old Style* and *Northern Farmer, New Style.*[1]

The Brownings

One of the great love affairs of all times was that between Robert Browning and Elizabeth Barrett. Elizabeth, one of the Barretts of Wimpole Street, was an invalid, but she got up the strength to lift a pen and write a little compliment to Browning about one of his poems. Browning, who thought anyone who liked his poetry couldn't be all bad, rushed over to see her. She read Browning some of her own poems and he opened the windows, partly to let in some fresh air and partly to show his muscles.[2] After a few more visits, he suddenly picked up Elizabeth and carried her off to Italy.[3] In return for all this, Elizabeth wrote *Sonnets from the*

[1] Lines such as "Wheer 'asta beän saw long and meä liggin' 'ere aloän" and "Me an' thy muther, Sammy, 'as beän a-talkin' o' thee" are thought to have influenced Rudyard Kipling, James Whitcomb Riley, and Edgar A. Guest.

[2] The windows hadn't been opened for years, and were stuck. The Victorians, who were afraid of fresh air, were deep thinkers but shallow breathers.

[3] Browning carried Elizabeth's pet spaniel, too, and was probably glad it wasn't a wolfhound or a Saint Bernard.

Elizabeth and Robert

Portuguese, in which she counted (and recounted) all the ways she loved Robert. Robert called them "the finest sonnets written in any language since Shakespeare's." Actually he thought them better than Shakespeare's, but tried not to be prejudiced because they were by his wife and about him.

Browning had enormous vitality. His health was such that doctors hoped it was not infectious. Had everyone been like him, the medical profession would have withered away. His only surgery was when he had "Italy" engraved on his heart, in a moment of whimsy. The ordinary person would have been satisfied to have had it tattooed on his arm.

He was also an optimist, even going so far as to think everyone would read the whole of *The Ring and the Book,* in which he tells the same story ten times.

He was not, however, much of an ornithologist. In *Pippa Passes*, for instance, he says "The lark's on the wing" instead of "The wing's on the lark."

Some of Browning's lines are puzzling. In *Andrea del Sarto* he maintains that "A man's reach should exceed his grasp," which is something you should try sometime, but not out where people can see you. And then there is his "Grow old along with me," which is almost impossible if you were born after 1889, the year Browning died. His

> Oh, to be in England
> Now that April's there

makes sense if you change the next two lines slightly to read:

> Be sure, though, that a raincoat
> And overshoes you wear.[1]

As for *Sordello*, Browning said that only he and God understood it, and some give this as evidence of Browning's faith in God.

Browning's dramatic monologues are said to be "like hearing one end of a telephone conversation." There is something snoopy about it, as you listen to the Duke telling someone about his last Duchess or Fra Lippo Lippi talking to a person named Zooks. "Zooks, what's to blame?" he says at one point. And then, at the end of the poem, simply "Zooks!" Apparently Zooks hung up on him.

[1] What Browning had in mind about England in April is that this is before the American tourists get there, along in June.

Charles Dickens

Charles Dickens was fortunate in having an unhappy childhood and a father who spent a good deal of time in debtors' prison. Otherwise he would not have had the material for *Oliver Twist*, *David Copperfield*, *Little Dorrit*, *Bleak House*, and *Hard Times*. Some other explanation must be found, however, for *A Tale of Two Cities*. Dickens, alas, had no first-hand knowledge of life in the Bastille, decapitation by the guillotine, or other exciting events of the French Revolution, since he had not yet been born.[1]

Probably the most formative experience of Dickens' youth was his employment in a blacking factory, pasting labels on bottles. Looking at those bottles of blacking, day after day, he naturally began to think about the darker aspects of life.[2] He was in school only briefly, but long enough to learn about Caning, a prerequisite for courses in Flogging and Starvation required of persons obtaining a teaching credential in those days. When a schoolmaster had a name like Wackford Squeers, in *Nicholas Nickleby*, he had to take it out on someone.

Not only Squeers but others had names that must have been hard to live with. Consider Bumble, Quilp, Scrooge, Smike, Heep, Gamp, Swiveller, Jellyby, and Gride. Dickens roamed the streets of London looking for people with odd names. "London," says one critic,

---

[1] It has been said that Dickens "drew on his father" when he was depicting Mr. Micawber in *David Copperfield*. His father was a very patient man.

[2] A bluing factory would also have been depressing.

"was Dickens' laboratory—the people, the food, the drink, the very smells." But if Dickens stood on the street corner sniffing, his readers are usually sniffling. "He tugs on the heartstrings," we are told, and the heartstrings seem to be attached to the tear ducts and to whatever it is that makes a lump in the throat. A good example is Dickens' masterful description of the death of Little Nell, in *The Old Curiosity Shop*. Here is the passage, stripped of nonessentials:

For she was dead. . . . She was dead. . . . She was dead. Dear, gentle, patient, noble Nell was dead. . . . She was dead, and past all help, or need of it. . . . She had been dead two days. . . . They did not know that she was dead at first.[1]

[1] There was something, perhaps the fact that she had stopped breathing, that finally made them suspicious.

Dickens gained such fame with *The Pickwick Papers*, *David Copperfield*, and other works, that he went to America. He traveled all over the country, reading his works aloud to people who were unable to read but loved being read to, especially by the author himself.[1]

William Makepeace Thackeray

Despite his middle name, Thackeray got into a fight at school that left him with a bashed-in nose. This is thought to have contributed to his dislike for snobs, who could look down their noses farther than he could. Though Thackeray did not again become involved in fisticuffs, he contributed to *Punch*.

It may also have been his embarrassment with that

[1] For a fuller treatment of Dickens, see *The Classics Reclassified*. I forget the name of the author.

middle name that led him to write under such pseudonyms as Charles James Yellowplush, George Savage Fitz-Boodle, and Michael Angelo Titmarsh. He even did a little painting as Théophile Wagstaff.[1] Finally, however, after experimenting with William M. Thackeray and W. M. Thackeray, he became reconciled to his full name, which was a relief to reviewers who had been asking, "Who is Ikey Solomons?" and "Who in the world is Major Goliah O'Grady Gahagan?"

In his early works Thackeray was mostly concerned with scoundrels, rogues, and thieves. As he matured, he turned more to the upper classes where, according to one critic, "he was preoccupied by the tufthunters." Never has the tuft been so assiduously hunted as in *Pendennis, The Newcomes,* and *Vanity Fair.* There are many kinds of tufts, and the tuft Thackeray's characters were after was more likely the gold tassel worn by titled students at Oxford and Cambridge than, say, the Malpighian tuft, a coil of capillaries in the kidney.

Vanity Fair is a peculiar novel in that it has no hero.[2] Thackeray makes up for this, however, by having two heroines, Becky Sharp and Amelia Sedley. The story concerns the ups and downs of these two women. Becky Sharp has a better time of it, since she is richly endowed with the qualities most useful in getting ahead in the world: ambition, unscrupulousness, and immorality.[3]

One of the great scenes in *Vanity Fair* is when

[1] The art critics were confounded. "Confound them!" Thackeray said.

[2] See also the opening of *Don Juan,* where Byron says, "I want a hero." Heroes seem to have been in short supply in those days.

[3] Becky is not only sharp but hard.

Becky's husband, Rawdon Crawley, catches Becky in a compromising situation with Lord Steyne. (He is just about to kiss her hand.) After an insulting remark from Steyne, who has paid cash for everything he is getting, this is the way it goes:

> Rawdon Crawley, springing out, seized him by the neckcloth, until Steyne, almost strangled, writhed, and bent under his arm. "You lie, you dog!" said Rawdon. "You lie, you coward and villain." And he struck the peer twice over the face with his open hand, and flung him bleeding to the ground.

What is notable is the restraint of Rawdon, the wronged husband, who strikes Lord Steyne with his open hand instead of making a fist, and hits him only two times at that. But apparently Steyne, who was elderly and dissipated, bled easily.

"Many attempts have been made to compare

Thackeray and Dickens as novelists," says one critic, "but the two authors are so different that this would be as much to the purpose as to compare chalk with cheese." What this critic does not say is which author is which.

The Brontës

Everyone knows about the Brontë sisters, but not so many know that the family name was originally Prunty or Brunty. The girls' father changed it because he was fascinated, as everyone else is, by those two little dots over the "e." Patrick Prunty or Brunty or Brontë was perpetual curate of Haworth, which means that he could have kept the job forever if he hadn't had the bad luck to die.

Haworth, where Charlotte, Emily, and Anne lived, was situated amidst what is variously described as "the bleak, cheerless Yorkshire valley," "the harsh moorlands of Yorkshire," and "the wild, windswept moors." It was the sort of place that got a poor press, and needed an active Chamber of Commerce.[1] The people of the region are described as "hard-bitten and suspicious," and those who had been bitten hard by whatever bit them had a right to be suspicious. It could happen again.

The rectory in which the girls lived was not exactly a fun place. Their father was a tyrant. Their mother and

[1] One biographer of the Brontës writes of their surroundings as "the gray, naked village . . . the small house, naked and gray . . . the graveyard with tombstones gray and naked." For the Victorian period, this was a lot of nakedness, gray or not.

Not a fun place

two sisters died of tuberculosis. Their brother Branwell
was a confirmed drunkard.[1] But the three sisters
livened things up by writing stories and poems which
they read aloud in the evenings, trying to drown out the
mournful sound of the wind in the moors. Finally they
published a volume of poems by Currer, Ellis, and Acton Bell. Currer was Charlotte, Ellis was Emily, and
Acton was Anne. Each pen name started with the same
letter as the author's real name. Clever as this was, the
book had a somewhat disappointing sale. It sold only
two copies.[2]

Undiscouraged by the lack of excitement over their

[1] Confirmed by friends, relatives, and pub owners. One biographer calls Branwell "sottish," but he was really Irish. It might
be added that he also took opium and went mad.

[2] One of the three authors must not have bought a copy.

poetry, the sisters turned to writing novels. The best
known of these are Charlotte's *Jane Eyre* and Emily's
Wuthering Heights. Anne was less successful, her *The
Tenant of Wildfell Hall* rarely appearing on the Required Reading List. But if it is true, as one critic says of
the two lovers, Helen and Gilbert, that at one point
"their relations were ruptured," it is a wonder the novel
has not been more popular. There is something compel-
lingly gruesome about a ruptured relation.

Jane Eyre and *Wuthering Heights* are said to have
given Victorian readers their first taste of romance and
passion.[1] *Jane Eyre* concerns a penniless, mistreated
orphan who becomes a governess in the household of
Mr. Rochester, a moody gentleman given to strange

[1] They smacked their lips, but not loud enough for anyone to
hear.

antics, such as dressing up as a gypsy fortune teller and sending telepathic messages instead of telegrams. Nonetheless Jane falls in love with him and would have married him but for the discovery that the raving maniac on the third floor is—his wife! Everything comes out all right, however, when the house burns down and burns the crazy wife with it. It would have been even better had Mr. Rochester not tried to rescue his wife from the roof, during the fire, and been blinded in the process. Two years after his marriage to Jane he regained the sight of one eye, which though not as good as regaining the sight of two eyes after one year was still an improvement. Aside from all the romance and passion, one of the virtues of the novel is the realistic dialogue, as when Jane exclaims: "The human and fallible should not arrogate a power with which the divine and perfect alone can be safely entrusted."

Wuthering Heights is even wilder and more passionate. Without going into the details of the story, involving a really unpleasant fellow, Heathcliff, who finally dies in the last chapter with a sneer on his face, let us comment on the appropriateness of the title. "Wuthering" is a dialect word, commonly encountered in the Brontë country, meaning stormy weather. If, when you are wandering around the Yorkshire moors on an ugly day, you happen to meet a hard-bitten native, you might say to him pleasantly, "Looks a bit wuthering, doesn't it?" But don't expect a reply.

Charlotte was the last of the six children to die and the only one to marry. There was something about her that appealed to preachers. After two of them proposed to her, she finally married a third, worn down by all the asking. In fact she was so worn down that she died a few months later, at the age of thirty-eight.[1]

George Eliot

George Eliot was born Mary Ann Evans, and those who saw her, with her square jaw and enormous head, agree that she did the right thing in changing her name from Mary to George. It was her large head that attracted Charles Bray, an amateur phrenologist, who at their first meeting asked, "Do you mind if I feel your bumps?" In addition to feeling bumps, Bray was always bumping into feelings, because he wrote books about free love that annoyed many a Victorian. What annoyed them was that they hadn't heard about this new arrangement before getting themselves locked into a marriage.

"George Eliot was essentially two people," writes one biographer, giving comfort to those who thought they had double vision. Perhaps stimulated by Charles Bray,[2] George Eliot moved in with George Henry Lewes. Since Lewes was married, they were unable to live as man and wife and had to make do as man and man. If there were not two George Eliots, at any rate there were two Georges. "Bring me my slippers,

[1] The lives of the Brontës are even more depressing than their books.
[2] More by his writings than by his feeling the bumps on her head.

George Eliot

George," one would say. "Yes, George," the other would reply.

After the death of George Henry Lewes, George Eliot, then sixty, married a man twenty years her junior. At last it was possible for George to live with someone as man and wife (George was the wife), though many thought it was more like mother and son.

It was while she was living in sin with George Henry Lewes that George Eliot wrote *Silas Marner*, a highly moral novel. Lewes is said to have "discovered and roused her creative gift," perhaps one time when he was just fiddling around. The idea for *Adam Bede* came from a story told her by her aunt, "who had once comforted through her last hours a poor thing condemned to be hanged for making way with her illegitimate baby." How the mother made way (or whey) with the baby is not told, though the recipe would be interesting and useful.[1]

Bulwer-Lytton said he thought the defects of *Adam Bede* were the use of dialect and the marriage of Adam. "I would have my teeth drawn," George Eliot said, "rather than give up either." She was a determined woman.[2] Of *Romola* it is said that "No other of her books ever cost such pains," presumably to the reader, trying to follow the plot of this novel as it wanders through the crowded streets of Florence.

At the height of George Eliot's fame,[3] people considered it an honor to be invited to one of her famous Sunday afternoons at home. One man recalls having attended such a gathering as a special treat when he was ten years old. He was "led into the presence of the gray sibyl enthroned at the end of the room, allowed to touch the tips of her fingers, and then taken away." Apparently he was considered too young for a handshake. Anyhow, it was something to tell his grandchildren, if he could get them to listen.

[1] It would fit nicely into Swift's *A Modest Proposal*.

[2] Whether she meant having her teeth pulled or having a picture drawn of them is not clear. The latter might have been more of a sacrifice.

[3] A contemporary critic called her "the greatest genius since Shakespeare."

George Eliot's last work, a volume of essays called *The Impressions of Theophrastus Such*, never attained widespread popularity despite the catchy title.

Other Victorians

Space does not permit discussion of such Eminent Victorians as Thomas Babington Macaulay, John Henry Newman, and Walter Savage Landor.[1] The last named, however, brings to mind a deathless couplet with which we conclude this chapter:

> Walter Savage Landor
> Never stooped to and/or.

[1] Lack of space is not the only reason for avoiding these writers. To be honest, the author is tiring. And so, probably, is the reader.

XIV

The Pre-Raphaelites

THE Pre-Raphaelite Brotherhood was made up of artists and writers who, "finding that the wine of imaginative writing had become watered in England, set out to crush anew in a fiery vintage what Keats had called 'joy's grape.'" It was probably all that stomping in the vats that produced what were called "purple patches." The Pre-Raphaelites published some of their works in *The Germ*, a magazine that lasted only four numbers. Subscribers may have thought it was a medical journal and were disappointed to find no health hints.

The Pre-Raphaelites were called Pre-Raphaelites because they thought things were better in art and literature before Raphael. Since Raphael was born in 1483, this was none too complimentary to Michelangelo (only eight years old when Raphael was born, and not yet doing his best work) and Shakespeare. To the Pre-Raphaelites, the Middle Ages were the Good Old Days, with their plagues, serfdom, tyranny, superstition, and religious persecution. The Brotherhood felt cheated by substitution of the materialism and ugliness of the machine age.[1]

[1] Also people were living longer, and this gave them more time to worry about the way things were going.

Pre-Raphaelite

Dante Gabriel Rossetti

Rossetti was both a painter and a poet. There could be nothing wrong with this except, as has been said, "Rossetti painted in his verse and sang in his pictures." Sometimes, it appears, he got the tools of his trade mixed up and wrote a sonnet with his brush, deriving a certain aesthetic satisfaction from colorfully dotting an "i" or crossing a "t." This is probably what the critic had in mind when he referred to "word painting" in Rossetti's poetry.

Rossetti's favorite theme was love, and he found his ideal image of a woman in Elizabeth Siddal, a clerk in a milliner's shop. She looked so good modeling hats that he got her to pose for him without a hat, or anything else. Then, satisfied that he knew what he was getting, he married her. In his sonnets he described what appealed to him about her, such as her "sultry hair," her "high-bosomed beauty," and her fingers "like rosy blooms." [1] Obviously she had been wasting her talents selling hats.

Two years after their marriage Elizabeth died. Rossetti was so distraught that he buried the manuscript of a new book of poems with her. However seven years later, after thinking it over, he had the poems exhumed and published them. After all, Elizabeth couldn't read them, down there in that poor light.

Rossetti's most famous poem is *The Blessed Damozel*, written when he was nineteen and, like others his age, preoccupied with death. It tells of a blessed damozel who is leaning over a bar in Heaven.[2] Her robe is all unfastened in front and, as Rossetti says, she has leaned there

> Until her bosom must have made
> The bar she leaned on warm.

Or, to look at it another way, it must have made her bosom cold. Anyhow, she has been in Heaven ten years and is impatient for her lover to die and join her. Whether she has been leaning over the bar all that time, with three lilies in her hand and seven stars in her hair, Rossetti does not say. But she is getting tired of waiting, and holding those flowers. It never occurs to her that her lover may already have died and gone elsewhere.

[1] He also says her fingers glowed like gold. He had her fingers on his brain or, as he says elsewhere, on his brows and on his soul.

[2] Some will find it hard to believe that there is a bar in the place, or a bartender.

Toward the end of his life Rossetti began to put on weight. He was terribly upset by an article in which he was referred to as a member of the Fleshy School of Poetry.

Christina Rossetti

Christina Rossetti was Dante's sister.[1] She was the only woman in the Brotherhood, and must have felt a little out of place. She refused to marry the man she loved, because he would not change his religion, and in consequence was despondent the rest of her life. Had she changed her own religion or married someone else, we would never have had such beautifully morbid or

[1] Dante Rossetti, that is.

Christina
Rossetti

morbidly beautiful poems as *When I Am Dead, My Dearest* and *The Heart Knoweth Its Own Bitterness.* Christina thought from an early age that death was imminent, and was as surprised as anyone that she lived to be sixty-four.[1]

Yet Christina had her happy moments, as in *A Birthday,* when she says, "My heart is like a singing bird." Trying again, she says, "My heart is like an appletree." And yet again, "My heart is like a rainbow shell." It would have been perplexing for a heart specialist had she replied in this way when he asked her, "Now tell me what seems to be the matter."

Goblin Market is Christina's most famous poem. She originally called it *A Peep at the Goblins,* but her brother Dante, annoyed by her constant chattering about death, may have said, "Not another peep out of you." The poem is about two sisters, Laura and Lizzie, who are tempted by goblins to eat their fruit. Laura finally gives in and eats some, but then sickens and is about to die because she is unable to get any more fruit, the goblins having disappeared. There is something habit-forming about the fruit and something very sly about the goblins.[2] To save her sister by giving her a second taste of the fruit and yet to keep from getting hooked herself, Lizzie seeks out the goblins and goads them into throwing fruit at her. Then she runs home and lets Laura lick the fruit off her face. "Hug me, kiss

[1] In *Looking Forward* she eagerly looks forward to dying, being buried, and having plants grow out of her. "Barren through life, but in death bearing fruit" is the way she expresses this interesting idea of having flowers and berries for offspring.

[2] Or fruit pushers.

me, suck my juices," Lizzie says in a rather disgusting scene. Laura swarms all over her, eating the fruit that is stuck in her ears and everywhere. This done, Laura quickly gets well, and Lizzie is spared the chore of washing her face.

There is supposed to be a moral in all this, perhaps that it is nice to have a sister who is willing to let her face be used as a plate.

William Morris

William Morris is probably the only English poet to have a chair named after him.[1] The Morris chair is an easy chair with an adjustable back and cushions. Morris himself, however, was far too busy to sit, being a manufacturer, decorator, painter, publisher, poet, and crusading Socialist. One of his most important activities was in connection with the Society for the Protection of Ancient Buildings. If anyone raised a hand to strike a helpless old building, Morris and his friends would rush in and would form a protective cordon around the place.

Morris hated ugliness. "I would have nothing in my home," he said, "that I do not know to be useful or believe to be beautiful." He started decorating his home by marrying Jane Burden, an attractive young woman who went nicely with the furniture.

A do-it-yourself type, Morris set up looms for weav-

---

[1] Other than an endowed professorship at a university.

Morris and chair

ing tapestry, had his own printing press, and designed stained glass, metalwork, and carpets. He often went to factories, where he lectured to workers about the joy of working with their hands, and they quit work to stand around and listen. Nothing gave him so much pleasure as watching the flow of honest sweat or examining a splendid handful of callouses.[1] He pled with workers to live with beauty in their homes, as he did, and caused many a worker to go home and look critically at his wife. Always he urged the return to medieval ways of work, involving long hours, hazardous working conditions, and confiscation of the products of toil by an overlord or the State. He thought this could best be achieved through Socialism.

The medieval in Morris's writing appears in such a poem as *The Defence of Guenevere,* in which Queen

[1] It was Browning, though, who wrote the famous line about "The first fine callous rapture."

Guenevere defends herself against some nasty charges made by Gawain. Guenevere confesses that she and Launcelot kissed, but everything else, she says, is a lie. Her description of that innocent little kiss shows how they did such things in the Middle Ages:

> When both our mouths went wandering in one way,
> And aching sorely, met among the leaves;
> Our hands being left behind strained far away.

It was all very casual and accidental, the two mouths just wandering around and happening to meet. The aching and soreness was caused by rubbing against leaves along the way. And we can imagine Guenevere exclaiming happily, "Look, Launcelot. No hands!" In fact both of the lovers left their hands far behind, perhaps in a pile of leaves, too busy with their lips to notice.[1]

The reader will be glad to know that the definitive edition of Morris's works runs to twenty-four volumes.

Algernon Charles Swinburne

Algernon Charles Swinburne is described, during his Oxford days, as "small and slight of stature, with an aureole of gold-red hair and a green-blue Pre-Raphaelite eye." Whether he had only one eye, or only one eye was of this peculiar sort, we are left to conjecture.

Though some of the things he wrote shocked the Victorians, and he even entitled one poem *On the Broads*,

---

[1] It might be added that Guenevere defends herself in terza rima, something seldom done in court these days.

Swinburne

he never married. He seems to have been too busy reading French, Greek, and Latin literature to do much with love except write about it.[1]

Swinburne was influenced by both the Bible and the Greeks, and had a difficult time choosing between Heaven and Hellenism. In addition to poetry and literary criticism, he wrote closet drama, even though it played to small audiences and the air was none too good and clothes hangers got in the way. Perhaps his most remarkable talent, as noted by one critic, was his ability "to make words sing." This took patience, especially with some of the little words that were shy and had to be coaxed.

Swinburne wrote some great lines. Among those that linger in one's mind are:

[1] And that green-blue Pre-Raphaelite eye may have frightened off the girls when he got up close.

I shall never be friends again with roses.[1]

O sad kissed mouth, how sorrowful it is!

I wish we were dead together today.

Villon, our sad bad glad mad [2] brother's name! [3]

I am sick of singing.

It is perhaps as a poet of love that Swinburne excelled. After you have thought back over the love lyrics of Spenser, Sidney, Shakespeare, Burns, and Byron, consider the psychological insight and the depth of passion achieved by Swinburne in *An Interlude*. Long centuries of striving by men of genius have finally brought us to this:

> And the best and the worst of this is
> That neither is most to blame,
> If you have forgotten my kisses
> And I have forgotten your name.

Both of the lovers seem to have been a little absent-minded. But kisses and names aside, practically everyone has forgotten the poem.

[1] Trying to shake hands, Swinburne had got a thorn in his thumb.

[2] Our poet was obviously using a rhyming dictionary.

[3] It was an odd family. Swinburne also claimed that Sappho was his sister, even though she lived around 600 B.C.

XV

Conclusion

THOUGH it had suffered a severe blow, English literature continued after the Pre-Raphaelites. For instance there is Thomas Hardy, an author who, according to one critic, "embraced most of the Victorian era and more than a quarter of the twentieth century." In addition to this feat, Hardy wrote novels in which he somehow managed to make everything come out for the worst. *The Return of the Native* has a typical Hardy ending: Mrs. Yeobright is bitten by a poisonous adder, her son Clym stumbles over her body,[1] and Eustacia and Wildeve drown. Egdon Heath, where man is always struggling against Fate,[2] is the gloomiest place since the Brontës' moors.[3]

Then there is Walter Pater. A lover of beauty, he thought people should spend every minute looking at works of art. It never occurred to him that some who

---

[1] But breaks no bones, thus providing one of the happier moments in the novel.

[2] And losing.

[3] If you find *The Return of the Native* depressing, perhaps you had better not read *Jude the Obscure*. The scene where Little Father Time hangs the two children and himself is only for the hardy.

Hardy people

look eagerly from side to side as they walk through an art museum are looking for a place to sit down. Though he was called a hedonist, an impressionist, and even a neo-pagan, he went right ahead, undaunted, and wrote such works as *Studies in the History of the Renaissance* and *Marius the Epicurean*. This latter work, which took him six years, is called "an imaginary portrait carried to the length of a novel." Carrying an imaginary portrait even a short distance requires a special talent.

At the end of the nineteenth century we have such writers as Robert Louis Stevenson, who was sickly, and Oscar Wilde, who was sickening. Stevenson traveled to America and to the South Seas in search of his health but, though he looked everywhere, was unable to find it. Oscar O'Flahertie Fingal Wills Wilde [1] tried hard

[1] Or Sebastian Melmoth, as he called himself after he got out of jail. Wilde was not only a queer bird but a jailbird.

A lily in his hand

not to avoid attention. Dressed in velveteen knee breeches, he always had a lily in his hand and a *bon mot* on his tongue.[1] He is known for both his pose and his poetry.

Mention should also be made of Rudyard Kipling, whom one critic calls "a champion of the British empire," without indicating whether in boxing, wrestling, cricket, or what. At any rate Kipling would never have been seen carrying a lily, just as Oscar Wilde would never have written a line like " 'E squatted in the scrub an' 'ocked our 'orses." [2]

Nor should we overlook such writers as George Bernard Shaw, who despite his beard gave us the word Shavian. Or John Galsworthy, who in *The Forsyte Saga* proved how many novels you can write about one family if you keep at it. Or Teodor Josef Konrad Korzeniowski, also known as Joseph Conrad, whose novels of the sea "describe the heroic men who walk the decks and heave round at a capstan," though they are not heroic enough to walk a few more steps and heave over the side.

Hurrying past such writers as A. E. Housman, who is best known for saying "one-and-twenty" instead of "twenty-one," [3] John Masefield, who never recovered

[1] The lily may have been intended as a symbol of the flowering of civilization. Then again, he may have been looking for a vase.

[2] In his *Jungle Book* Kipling succeeds in making animals talk like human beings, and in *Barrack Room Ballads* he makes human beings talk like animals.

[3] Oddly, it was not A. E. Housman but George William Russell who was called "A. E."

from a bad case of sea fever, William Butler Yeats, who if he had been Keats would have pronounced his name Kates, and Virginia Woolf, who wallowed about for years in a stream of consciousness and finally drowned herself, we come to T. S. Eliot.

When Eliot, who was born in St. Louis, Missouri, became an English author, he posed serious questions for literary historians. Should he be included in English literature or in American literature? And what do you do with Aldous Huxley and W. H. Auden?

There was no such confusion about Chaucer, who died ninety-two years before Columbus discovered America.

About the Author

A graduate of Pomona College and a Ph.D. from Harvard, Richard Armour taught English literature for thirty-eight years at such institutions as the University of Texas, Northwestern University, Wells College, the University of Freiburg, the University of Hawaii, Scripps College, and the Claremont Graduate School. He was also Dean of the Faculty at Scripps College. Though his specialties have long been Chaucer and the Romantic Poets, on which he has written scholarly books and articles, he has also taught the traditional sophomore Survey of English Literature. He is now Emeritus, which he translates as "out of merit." He has lectured or been guest-in-residence on more than two hundred campuses, has held research fellowships in England and France, and has lectured as an American Specialist for the State Department in both Europe and Asia.

After several heavily footnoted books, which he says he wrote "to get promoted," he turned to the satires and spoofs of scholarship which have won him critical acclaim and a wide readership. These books have been in such varied fields as history (*It All Started with Co-*

lumbus, It All Started with Europa, Our Presidents, etc.), medicine (*It All Started with Hippocrates, The Medical Muse*), golf (*Golf Is a Four-Letter Word*), adolescence (*Through Darkest Adolescence*), and higher education (*Going Around in Academic Circles*). He has also written several books of light verse and half a dozen books for children, the latest being *On Your Marks,* a book in verse about the punctuation marks, with a foreword by Ogden Nash. His satires and parodies of literature, well known to students and teachers, include *Twisted Tales from Shakespeare, The Classics Reclassified, Punctured Poems,* and *American Lit Relit. English Lit Relit* is his thirty-ninth book. He has also contributed more than six thousand pieces of prose and verse to some two hundred magazines in the United States and England.

Dr. Armour is married, has a son and daughter, and lives in Claremont, California.

About the Illustrator

Campbell Grant, who has illustrated ten of Richard Armour's books, was with Walt Disney for twelve years as a character creator and story man. During World War II he worked with Frank Capra on documentaries. He is the illustrator of many books for children and adults and has done the drawings for the book version of many Disney films. Since 1960 he has been actively interested in archaeology, and has recorded and made paintings of the aboriginal rock paintings in the Santa Barbara mountains and published many articles on the subject. In 1965 his first book was published, *The Rock Paintings of the Chumash*. It was picked as one of the top 25 books of the year for outstanding design at the 1966 American Association of University Presses book show. Later he broadened the scope of the study to include the rock art of North America, and the recently published *Rock Art of the American Indian* is the definitive book on the subject. He teaches art at a nearby private school, travels widely, and is active in conservation matters. Living idyllically on a ranch near Santa Barbara, he raises avocados and has a talented writer-wife and four children.